# PETERSON'S

# SAT*

# WORD FLASH

## The Quick Way to Build Verbal Power for the New SAT—and Beyond

### Joan Carris

*SAT IS A REGISTERED TRADEMARK OF THE COLLEGE ENTRANCE EXAMINATION BOARD, WHICH WAS NOT INVOLVED IN THE PRODUCTION OF, AND DOES NOT ENDORSE, THIS PRODUCT.

## Peterson's
Princeton, New Jersey

**Library of Congress Cataloging-in-Publication Data**

Carris, Joan.
    SAT word flash : the quick way to build verbal power for the SAT—and beyond / Joan Carris.—2nd ed.
        p.    cm.
    Includes index.
    ISBN 1-56079-850-5
    1. Scholastic Aptitude Test—Study guides.    2. English language—Examinations—Study guides.    3. Vocabulary tests—Study guides.    I. Title.
    LB2352.57.C367    1997
    378.1'662—dc21                                                          97-8917
                                                                            CIP


Printed in the United States of America

10 9 8 7 6 5 4

# CONTENTS

Vital Information     **1**

What You Already Know—A Quick Review     **5**

List of Abbreviations     **19**

  **1.** A Laudable List of Verbs     17

  **2.** Down with Bombast!     23

  **3.** Sycophants Have Brown Noses     28

  **4.** How Germane, My Dear     33

  **5.** Snoots Up     38

**Review: Lists 1–5**     **43**

  **6.** Verbs to Heed     48

  **7.** Beware a Parsimonious Predecessor     53

  **8.** That's Me!     58

  **9.** Pairs of Popular Opposites     63

**10.** The Blues     69

**Review: Lists 6–10**     **74**

**11.** Vacillate Not!     78

**12.** How Much is a Dearth?     83

**13.** An Eclectic Collection     89

**14.** Yakkety Yak     94

**15.** Wishy-Washy     99

**Review: Lists 11–15**     **104**

**16.** More Verbs to Love     108

**17.** An Esteemed Assortment     113

**18.** Feeling Good     118

**19.** Mighty Obvious Opposites     123

**20.** Compliment? Not!     128

**Review: Lists 16–20**     **133**

**21.**  Ah, the Prudent Puritans                    137

**22.**  Out of this World                            142

**23.**  Big, Fat, Glorious Adjectives                147

**24.**  Goulash                                      152

**25.**  A Is for Arbitrary                           157

**Review: Lists 21–25**                              **162**

**26.**  Bolster, Don't Carp                          166

**27.**  How Bizarre!                                 171

**28.**  Not Obsolete at All                          177

**29.**  Attitudes                                    182

**30.**  On the Dark Side                             187

**Review: Lists 26–30**                              **192**

**The Answers**                                      **196**

**Index of Words and Roots**                         **214**

# VITAL INFORMATION

This is not another boring introduction. The next few pages really DO contain vital information, just as the heading says.

## Do You Need to Pump Up Your Vocabulary?

Most people would like a big, strong vocabulary for about a zillion reasons, only one of which is needing an impressive SAT or PSAT score. And don't let anyone kid you—the verbal sections on SATs and PSATs are *vocabulary tests*. (So are most IQ tests.)

Remember that your language doesn't just say who you are, it *trumpets* who you are. Either you sound bright and well educated or you don't. You can't fool people—not for long anyway. There is no substitute for an educated vocabulary. Your language will shape your life; I absolutely guarantee it.

## Honest Talk About Learning

When you're very young, learning happens all the time, and you don't even have to think about it. One day you're popping those little bits of cereal into your mouth, and the next day your saying "Cheerio, Cheerio!" and a proud parent is grinning from ear to ear. Nothing to it.

Well, you're older now, and the truth is that most learning involves work. The more complex the subject, the more work it's apt to take. **But vocabulary is one of the EASIER things to learn if you go about it the right way.** Isn't that a relief? Also, people remember what they enjoy studying. We tried to build a great deal of FUN into this book.

## Analyze Yourself. How Do You Learn?

Ask yourself these few questions. Then you can use the answers to make learning the words in this book easier.

- *Do you learn best in the early morning?* What an awful thought. Still, half the world is like this.
- *Do you learn better in the late afternoon?* In the evening? When are you too sleepy to work well?
- *Do you learn best with music on or off?* Be careful here. Most of us learn well only when it's quiet.
- *Do you need to write something down to learn it?* I would have flunked history if I hadn't highlighted lines in the textbook and written a full outline of all we studied.
- *Do you need to hear something to remember it?* Over one third of us learn best through our ears.
- *Do you feel better about studying if you have iced tea or Coke*, etc., to keep you company?

1

- *Is learning more apt to happen if you work with a friend* or study group, or do you work best alone?
- *Do you learn more efficiently if you say* "I'm going to do this assignment in 30 minutes, no matter what"?

Think about all these topics. Where and when and how do you do your very best learning? You need to know.

## Why Learn the Words in This Book?

The words in this book are the *must know* words for SATs. As an SAT/PSAT coach, I've been keeping records for fifteen years of the words that stump kids over and over again. Those words are all here. On the SATs published since 1980, certain words occur regularly. THOSE WORDS are here, too.

Why do the same words appear again and again in most SAT prep books and on tests similar to SATs? Because these particular words really do the job. They are some of our most descriptive, specific adjectives—our most precise, active verbs—our information-packed nouns—yet none is overused or trite.

Words used all the time lose their punch. Let's take *sad*. Sara is sad about losing her boyfriend. Does that give you a vivid picture of Sara? No, and that's why we need *downcast, gloomy, sorrowful, disheartened, morose, anguished, wretched,* and all the others, each with its separate shades of meaning, so that we know EXACTLY how Sara feels.

## Who Needs This Many Words?

You do, if you want to go to college or if you want to be thought of as an intelligent person. Remember that you must have a respectable vocabulary to be a good reader, and about 90 percent of college work depends on reading comprehension. Also, competence in writing is required in college and on the job, and *only* good readers are good writers. Since you need to be a good reader AND writer (let's add good speaker too), a bigger vocabulary is obviously the first requirement.

Remember, too, that your aim in talking and writing is to communicate, not in a general way but very specifically. Accurate communication requires a large supply of words. If your boss asks you to analyze progress on a project, he won't appreciate "It's going, like, kinda okay, you know?"

Even if you're a math major or a computer techie, you'll need to communicate your knowledge effectively and persuasively to other people. Einstein had to explain to others the significance of $E = mc^2$.

*Enough!* you're hollering. Okay, because even if I gave you a hundred reasons for learning these words, it would still boil down to the real reason: *lifestyle choice.* Strong language skills will get you the job, and therefore the lifestyle that you want. Lousy language skills will limit your choices alarmingly.

So, think . . . Where do you want to go in life and how will you get there? We're agreed that an educated vocabulary is the first step. Now, how can you get one with a minimum of agony?

# How to Learn Every Word in This Book

*First, fire up your determination.* People who make things happen are determined people. Just wishing is never enough. If it were, you'd have a Porsche in your driveway.

Next, *try what I'm suggesting here.* Then, if it doesn't work, make your own plan for mastering these lists. We're only talking about 400 to 500 words, depending on how many synonyms you learn along the way.

1. **Flip through the book to get a feel for each lesson.** There are thirty lists of words, only twelve words each, plus two roots and their necessary words, for a total of sixteen words in each lesson. You'll know at least a couple on each list, so you'll actually be learning fourteen words at most. Every five lists, there's a review lesson to make sure you still know the words.

2. **Try this Three-Day Miracle Plan for each lesson:**

   **Day 1**—Read each word, its definition, and the example sentences. Read all the way through, because often a story will lead you from one word to the next. Concentrate on any word that seems hard to remember. After studying the roots and their example words, do Memory Fix, the first practice with words in each lesson.

   **Day 2**—Do the rest of the exercises. Write in this book. Highlight. Underline. Check any questions about pronunciation in a collegiate dictionary like *Webster's* or *Random House.*

   **Day 3**—Self-quiz. Write the new words on a separate piece of paper with a definition or synonyms for each. If you know them all, rent a movie with friends to celebrate. Tomorrow you can begin a new list.

3. **You'll need just a few minutes a day** for three months to learn every word in this book on our Three-Day Miracle Plan. That's just one summer—or late summer and early fall. If you can work faster, do it. If you're a slow worker, it would be smarter to learn fewer words thoroughly, so that you have them for life, rather than trying to cram in all the words, retaining hardly any.

4. **If you learn best in a group, form an SAT study group** with regular meeting times and assignments. Medical students do this to learn their most difficult subjects, and you can, too. Group learning is usually fun.

5. **Read . . . and read some more.** Nothing helps people to learn words like seeing them in context over and over again. (People who love to read always think SAT verbal sections are easy.) If you come across a word you don't know, ask someone who does, then *write the word and its definition in this book.* Or look up the unknown word in a dictionary.

   **Read magazines or newspapers** that are well written, such as *Sports Illustrated, The New York Times,* the *Christian Science Monitor,* the *Boston Globe,* the *Washington Post,* etc.

**Read books on topics you enjoy.** If it isn't pleasurable, you won't do it. Reading is supposed to be fun.

6. **Yes, use the dictionary.** It's your friend, and you need to have a solid relationship. Get a pocket dictionary to carry with you. All bright people act this way.

7. **Limit your TV time.** Unless you're trying to beef up your total of 18,000+ murders seen by graduation (the average for all high schoolers), punch the little OFF button and let the boob tube rest. Its vocabulary *stops* at the sixth-grade level, remember?

8. **Think about opposites.** Antonyms are useful memory tools. *Night* has much more meaning when contrasted with *day*. If you know that *joyful* is the opposite of *morose*, you'll remember what *morose* means even though you use it less often.

9. **Think about roots.** The etymology (word history + root) of a word is a vital clue to its meaning. You know that a *hydr*ant dispenses *water.* So if you *hydr*ate a substance, you're adding water. An an*hydr*ous compound has no water . . . and so on. Knowing roots is the key to the meaning of 60 to 70 percent of English words.

   Every root you learn is a kind of verbal gold. A root like *duc/duct* (lead, guide) is the basis for over 2,000 English words. *Gen* in *gen*tleman, *gen*esis, and in*gen*uous has spawned over 50 words, all of them favorites with SAT question-makers. *The roots you absolutely must know are in this book, two solid-gold roots per lesson.*

10. **How can you remember all the words?** Make flashcards. If law and medical students do it, then we should pay attention. Smart people do what works. Ask parents and friends to quiz you with the flashcards. Carry them with you in your pocket or purse. You'll be astounded at what you can learn in a few odd minutes here or there.

   **Use memory aids to fix words in your mind.** These are called *mnemonic devices.* Mne = *memory* as in a*mne*sia, a*mne*sty, and *mne*monics. (See what I mean about roots?) Draw a picture on your flashcards if it helps. Connect a person to a word. Make a silly sentence using the word you need to memorize. *Brusque Bob Baker barks at me.* Mnemonics work best when they're personal.

   Another great memory aid is writing. The old schoolmarm trick of "Write it ten times" was a trick that worked. It still does.

   *Try* all this, okay? If you're not learning words like crazy after a few weeks, devise methods that you like better. In other words, move through this book at your own pace, in your own way. You're acquiring an educated vocabulary to use the rest of your life. And while you're learning the new words, *use them!* That's the only way to keep them forever.

# WHAT YOU ALREADY KNOW— A QUICK REVIEW

Promise. This *will* be quick because you already know these critical bits of vocabulary. Just whip through this review, and you'll feel much happier about your vocabulary. These are terribly helpful clues to thousands of English words that you need, and you *really do know them*. They've just been hanging around in the back of your mind, waiting for you to call on them.

The two lessons here will take only 30 minutes each—probably the best hour you'll spend all week. *You're going to be amazed* at what you already know that will boost your score on any test involving words.

## Lesson A

How do smart people learn? They write information down, read what they've written, and say it out loud. They may repeat these three steps a few times, fixing the material in mind, and then they'll have it forever. So, get smart! Write these roots down, learn their definitions and those of the sample words, and you'll be taking a large step toward a bigger vocabulary.

**AQUA** and **HYDR** = water and **MAR** = sea, ocean

| | | |
|---|---|---|
| aquarium | hydrant | marine |
| aqualung | hydraulic | aquamarine |
| aquamarine | dehydrate | mariner |
| aqueduct | hydrolysis | maritime |
| | hydrogen | submarine |

So *aquamarine* (a pale turquoise-colored stone) really means "water of the sea," a perfect description.

**EGO** and **AUTO** = I, self

| | |
|---|---|
| ego | autocrat |
| egotist | autograph |
| superego | automobile |
| egocentric | autobiography |
| alter ego | autonomous |
| | autodidactic |

**BIO = life**

biology        biopsy        biography
autobiography  symbiosis

**MATER = mother** and **PATER = father**

| | |
|---|---|
| matron | paternal |
| maternal | patriot |
| matrimony | paternity |
| matriarchal | patriarchal |
| maternity | patrimony |

A *patriot*, therefore, is loyal to his *father*land.

**AUD/AUDIT = hear**

audition   audible   auditorium
inaudible  audience  audit

**SCRIB/SCRIPT** and **GRAPH/GRAM = to write**

| | |
|---|---|
| scribe | graphic |
| scribble | telegraph |
| inscribe | biography |
| describe | photography |
| prescribe | telegram |
| proscribe | mammogram |
| inscription | cardiogram |
| description | |

My *auto-bio-graphy*, the story of my life, is literally "writing my life." Three roots in one word.

**GE/GEO = earth** and **AGR = field, soil**

| | |
|---|---|
| geology | agriculture |
| geophysics | agronomy |
| geometry | agrarian |
| apogee | agrochemical |

**SCI** and **COGN/COGNI/GNO(S)** = **to know**

| | |
|---|---|
| science | cognizant |
| omniscient | cognate |
| prescient | incognito |
| conscious | recognize |
| | prognosis |
| | agnostic |

*Prescient* . . . a tough word, right? Not anymore. The prefix *pre* meaning "before" and the root *sci* give you the meaning. *Prescient* means "knowing ahead of time, able to foretell."

**VID/VIS** = **to see**

| | |
|---|---|
| video | evident |
| provide | vision |
| revise | advise |
| improvise | |

**CHRON** and **TEMPOR** = **time**

| | |
|---|---|
| chronology | tempo |
| synchronize | temporize |
| chronometer | temporary |
| anachronism | contemporary |
| | extemporaneous |

**SENS/SENT** = **to feel**

| | |
|---|---|
| sensible | resent |
| dissent | consent |
| sensual | presentiment |

A *presentiment* is "a foreboding," a "feeling before" something happens that you know what's about to happen. Another gift from the world of roots!

**CIV** = **citizen**

| | |
|---|---|
| civic | civil |
| civilian | civilization |
| civility | |

**FALL/FALS = to deceive, be not truthful**

| | |
|---|---|
| fallacy | fallacious |
| infallible | false |
| falsify | falsehood |

Vords from this root are *always* on SATs and PSATs!

**CYCL = circle**

| | |
|---|---|
| cycle | recycle |
| cyclical | tricycle |
| bicycle | Cyclops |

**NEG = to deny, not**

| | |
|---|---|
| negative | renege |
| renegade | abnegation |

And remember these incredibly useful prefixes? Read each one aloud slowly as a memory refresher.

**A/AN = not, without**

| | |
|---|---|
| anomaly | atrophy |
| amoral | agnostic |
| atheist | anonymous |
| amorphous | atypical |

**AB/ABS = from, away**

| | |
|---|---|
| absent | abhor |
| abstain | abrupt |
| abbreviate | abrasive |
| abdicate | abnormal |

(You knew you wanted to stay *away* from someone who was acting *ab*normal, right?)

**AC/AD/AF, etc. = to, toward, against**

| | |
|---|---|
| adhere | aggregate |
| addict | apportion |
| aspect | attend |

**ANTE/ANTI = before, previous**

| | | |
|---|---|---|
| anteroom | anticipate | antedate |
| antecedent | antebellum | anterior |

**ANTI = against, opposing**

antisocial   antithesis   antidote
antiseptic   antipathy   antibiotic

**BENE = good, well**

benefit         beneficial
beneficent    benefactor
benediction   benevolent

**CIRCU = around**

circuit          circuitous
circumspect   circumnavigate
circumvent    circumference

**CO/COL/COM, etc. = with, together**

collateral   cooperate     concede
coerce       collaborate   compassion
correlate    concur

**CONTRA/COUNTER = against, opposing**

contradict     counteract   countereffective
contraband   contrary

**DI/DIA = across, apart, through, between**

dilate        diaphragm
diameter    diaphanous
dialogue    dialectic

**DIS/DI/DIFF = away, apart, negative**

disparate       difference
diffuse          dissuade
disseminate   disperse

**EN/EM = in, among, within**

enliven      empathy   enhance
embarrass   embed      enforce

## MEMORY CHECK

To fix these important prefixes in your memory, fill in the missing info in this chart.

| Prefix | Meaning | Examples |
|---|---|---|
| **A/An** |  | atheist, anomaly, atypical |
|  | from, away |  |
| **DIS/DI/DIFF** |  |  |
|  | before, previous | anteroom, anticipate |
| **BENE** |  |  |
|  | around |  |
|  |  | diameter, dialogue, dilate |
| **ANTI** |  |  |
|  | against, opposing |  |
| **CO/COL/COM** |  | cooperate, concede, concur |

# Lesson B
. . . because you can never know too many prefixes!

**EPI = outside, over, outer**
epilogue    epidermis    epitaph
epiphany    epicenter

**EX/EXTRA/EXTER/EXTRO = out, outside, beyond**
expel        extrovert            external
extol        extraordinary

**HETERO = other**
heterodox    heterogeneous    heterosexual

**HOMO = same**
homogeneous    homophone    homosexual
homonym

**IN/IL/IM/IR = in, within or not, opposing**
internal        imply        indecent
intrinsic       imprint      inefficient
influx          irradiate    illegal
irreverent

**INTER = among, between**
interact    intervene    interdict    intersect

**INTRA/INTRO = inwardly, within**
intramural    intravenous    introduce    introvert

A wee cheer here for roots and prefixes. One who turns (*vert*) himself *out* for others (an outgoing personality) is an *extro*vert; the *intro*vert is turned *in*ward (may be an *intro*spective type), a less open individual by far.

**MACRO/MAG/MEGA/MAX = big, long**
macrocosm        macroeconomics
magnitude        magnanimous
maximum          megalomaniac

> **MAL = bad, badly**
> malady      malicious     malign
> malevolent  maleficent    malinger
> dismal      malaise

> **META/MET = change of, over, beyond**
> metaphor        metabolism
> metaphysics     metamorphism
> metastasize

## MEMORY CHECK 1

Try your hand at completing the following sentences.

1. The elephant wears his *epi*dermis on the _____.

2. A *hetero*geneous group is _____.

3. A naked ghost would be both _____ decent *and* _____ substantial, right?

4. Playing it to the *max* means _____.

5. We know *Male*ficent means trouble in "Sleeping Beauty" because she has such a _____ name.

6. Our favorite *meta*morphic critter is the butterfly, who _____ his form (*morph*) into one that can fly.

**MICRO = small**

microbe microscope microphone microcosm

**OMNI and PAN = all, entire**

omnivorous  panorama
omnipresent  panacea
omniscient  pandemic
 pandemonium
 pantheon

**ORTH = straight, right**

orthodox orthodontist orthopedic orthotics

**PAR/PARA = beside, next to**

paradox  paragon
parenthesis  paraphrase
paradigm  parasite

**PER = through, throughout or completely, wrongly**

persecute  permeate
perjury  permit
perturb  persiflage

**PERI = around, near**

perimeter periscope peripatetic periphery

**POST = after, following**

postpone posthumous postmortem posterior

**PRE = before**

predict  prefix
preordained  preliminary
pregnant  precipitate
precocious  predilection

PRO = for, forward, before, forth, favoring

| | |
|---|---|
| progress | promote |
| progenitor | prognosis |
| provision | promise |

RE/RETRO = back, again

| | |
|---|---|
| recoil | retreat |
| retain | retroactive |
| retrospect | recur |
| refer | rehearse |
| reiterate | remember |

## MEMORY CHECK 2

As before, fill in the missing boxes in the chart.

| Prefix | Meaning | Examples |
|---|---|---|
| | small | microbe, microphone, microcosm |
| **PRE** | | predict, prefix, preliminary |
| | straight, right | |
| **PER** | | permeate, permit |
| | around, near | periscope, perimeter, periphery |
| **PRO** | | |
| | after, following | |
| | | recoil, retreat, retroactive |
| **OMNI, PAN** | | |

**SE = apart, away from**

| | |
|---|---|
| seclude | segregate |
| secede | sequester |
| seduce | separate |

**SUB/SUC/SUF/SUG/SUM/SUP/SUS = under, below**

| | |
|---|---|
| subzero | submarine |
| succeed | suffuse |
| suggest | summon |
| suppose | suspend |

**SUPER/SUR = over, above, extra**

| | |
|---|---|
| superstar | superimpose |
| survey | surpass |
| superficial | surmount |

**SYL/SYM/SYN/SYS = together**

| | |
|---|---|
| syllable | symmetry |
| symphony | synergy |
| synopsis | synthesis |
| system | systolic |

**TELE = from afar**

telegram   telephone   telephoto   telescope   telemetry

**TRA/TRANS = across, beyond**

| | |
|---|---|
| traverse | travesty |
| trajectory | transport |
| transgress | transform |

**UN and IN = not, opposing**

| | |
|---|---|
| unwary | unequal |
| unmitigated | unsuspecting |
| indistinct | inequitable |

**WITH = against**

withhold   withstand   withdraw

## MEMORY CHECK 3

Time to put your knowledge of these prefixes to the test. Fill in the
blanks in the following sentences.

1.  If you *se*clude a criminal in order to *se*gregate him from society,
    you have _____ him from normal life.

2.  A *tele*phone brings you voices from _____.

3.  That long, cigar-shaped ship that stays "under the sea" for
    months at a time is rightly called a _____.

4.  A _____ store will provide
    _____ savings that will _____pass your
    wildest dreams. These stores truly are *over* and *above* all others,
    offering many *extras*.

5.  The purpose of _____chronizing our watches is so that we
    will be _____ in time (*chron*).

**Answers for this chapter begin on page 196.**

# A LAUDABLE LIST OF VERBS

---

**acquiesce • chastise • augment • condone • amass • disseminate • coalesce • concur • digress • laud • disperse • efface**

---

**ACQUIESCE** v. *to give in and agree peaceably; to assent, comply* n. acquiescence
When Dad set 1 a.m. as our curfew, my sister Amy and I *acquiesced* because we knew he meant business. For me, it's easier to *acquiesce* than to argue forever, which I hate.

**CHASTISE** v. *to scold severly or punish; castigate, censure*
Every day we *chastise* Dude, my insanely brave, five-pound Yorkshire terrier. But Meatloaf, Amy's sixteen-pound cat, has almost never been *chastised*, probably because she's too smart to get caught.

**AUGMENT** v. *to increase; to make something greater or bigger*
Dad said, "Ted, I'll *augment* your allowance for your senior year, in return for more help at home." That could mean major labor, but I have to *augment* my savings before college.

**CONDONE** v. *to overlook or pardon an offense; to excuse*
For too long, our family has *condoned* Dude's mad-dog tendencies. We keep making excuses for him, unlike my high school principal, who rarely *condones* misbehavior.

**AMASS** v. *to accumulate, collect; to gather, come together*
I don't need to *amass* a huge fortune, but a bit of extra money would be nice—for camping gear, of course. Whenever ours is *amassed* in one place, I see how much we need.

**DISSEMINATE** v. *to disperse or spread everywhere (knowledge or ideas) as if sowing seeds*
Our school paper, *The Central Times*, tries to *disseminate* the information all students need. As editor, I hope the paper also *disseminates* the spirit of Central High.

---

**CUR/CURR/COURS = to run, course**

cursory—*sketchy, not thorough; hasty or superficial*
  a *cursory* glance
  a regrettably *cursory* reading

precursor—*a forerunner that hints at the future; harbinger*
  the first robin, a welcome *precursor* of spring

Also: **cursive, excursion, current, curriculum, discourse, incur, cursor, occur, concur, discursive**

---

**COALESCE** v. *to mix or come together from separate elements*
Thoughts about my last editorial finally *coalesced* into one good idea. Amy couldn't believe I was actually writing about her play cast, a group of radically different kids that I saw *coalescing* into a supportive stage family.

**CONCUR** v. *to agree, assent; to approve; to coincide*
After much discussion, our family *concurred* on a camping site for next summer. Luckily, Dad's vacation time is *concurrent* with the best time to visit the park we selected.

**DIGRESS** v. *to wander off course in speaking or writing*
I often *digress* into related topics as I get into a speech. I think these *digressions* are humorous, but my teacher has started saying, "Ted, if you keep *digressing*, I'll mark you down. You must stay on target."

---

**MISS/MIT = to send**

emit—*to voice; to give off, as fumes or anger*
  *emitted* a low groan
  *emit* foul fumes
  *emission* standards

mission—*a definite job or task; the mission establishment itself (usually religious)*
  needing a clear *mission*
  the old adobe Jesuit *mission*

Also: **omit, omission, commit, commission, permit, permission, transmit, transmission, missive, missile**

---

**LAUD** v. *to praise, commend, acclaim, extol*
We rarely say, "You are to be *lauded* for that achievement" anymore, favoring the word praised or commended instead. But I often hear "What a *laudable* accomplishment."

**DISPERSE** v. *to spread all over; to disseminate;* also, *to fan out or scatter in a random way*
With promotion of school events as one goal, we *disperse* copies of *The Central Times* to each class. Most kids came to the recent basketball tournament and *dispersed* like so many bats afterward, flitting home to study for exams.

**EFFACE** v. *to erase or obliterate; to wear away (as by time)*
I'm counting on time to *efface* the memories of when I've made a total idiot of myself, just as weather has gradually *effaced* the harsh or exaggerated features of nature.

## List of Abbreviations

Take a minute to familiarize yourself with the following abbreviations, which are used in the vocabulary lessons.

| | | | | | |
|---|---|---|---|---|---|
| **n.** | noun | **s.** | singular | **L.** | Latin |
| **v.** | verb | **pl.** | plural | **Fr.** | French |
| **adj.** | adjective | **usu.** | usually | **Sp.** | Spanish |
| **adv.** | adverb | **lit.** | literally | **Gr.** | Greek |
| | | | | **Ger.** | Germanic |

## MEMORY FIX

To learn these new words, write each one on a sheet of paper. Also write a synonym or definition for each and say the words aloud as you work.

## FILL IN THE BLANKS

From the words in this chapter, select the one that best completes the meaning and logic of each phrase below. Note which tense or form of the word is required for sense.

1. wouldn't _____ unless I could yield with a clear conscience

2. can't possibly _____ that rude behavior

3. harsh weather that _____ the writing on the tomb

**4.** formal enough to say _____ instead of scold

**5.** an opinion that fortunately _____ with mine

**6.** "all glory, _____, and honor" goes the hymn

**7.** to _____ as much as possible, the goal of Scrooge McDuck

**8.** eager to _____ the number of qualified students

**9.** careful to focus on the problem and not _____

**10.** a thorough reading, please, not a _____ one

**11.** a rambling, _____ talk that put everyone to sleep

**12.** where the two paths _____ into one wider path

**13.** hope to _____ the news to as many as possible

**14.** quit milling around and _____ peaceably now

**15.** _____ a low cry of astonishment before falling silent

## ANALOGIES

Circle the one word pair in each list below that expresses the same relationship as the pair in capital letters.

**1. CHASTISE : MISBEHAVIOR**
   (A)  start : argument
   (B)  castigate : students
   (C)  laud : success
   (D)  represent : hope
   (E)  remunerate : reward

**2. FOOTPRINTS : EFFACE**
   (A)  scars : hide
   (B)  gulley : widen
   (C)  target : omit
   (D)  memorial : dedicate
   (E)  record : obliterate

3. **ACQUIESCE : YIELDING**
   (A) comply : hesitating
   (B) disperse : scattering
   (C) concur : running
   (D) emit : smelling
   (E) commit : halting

4. **PATH : STRAY**
   (A) lecture : digress
   (B) book : review
   (C) illness : recur
   (D) duties : remiss
   (E) elements : coalesce

5. **PARDON : OFFENSE**
   (A) amass : wealth
   (B) punish : wrongdoing
   (C) condone : error
   (D) censure : actions
   (E) disseminate : cheer

## MATCHING

Circle the two words or phrases that best explain the meaning of each of the words in bold type.

1. **acquiesce**
   (A) dispute
   (B) assent
   (C) drench
   (D) yield

2. **emit**
   (A) utter
   (B) voice
   (C) take in
   (D) abhor

3. **castigate**
   (A) scorn
   (B) chastise
   (C) scold
   (D) tie up

4. **precursor**
   (A) forerunner
   (B) patron
   (C) arbiter
   (D) harbinger

5. **amass**
   (A) ritual
   (B) accumulate
   (C) gather
   (D) Southern for "disaster"

6. **augment**
   (A) enlarge
   (B) add to
   (C) alter
   (D) price

7. **disperse**
   (A) avoid
   (B) strew around
   (C) arrange
   (D) disseminate

8. **coalesce**
   (A) join
   (B) roil around
   (C) come together
   (D) disturb

9. **efface**
   (A) embarrass
   (B) wear away
   (C) erase
   (D) expose

10. **cursory**
    (A) sketchy
    (B) cautious
    (C) ignorant
    (D) hasty

**Answers for this chapter begin on page 197.**

# LIST 2

# DOWN WITH BOMBAST!

---

banal • terse • raconteur • euphemism • succinct•
hackneyed • bombast • articulate • laconic •
hyperbole • lampoon • platitude

---

**BANAL** adj. *commonplace and stale, not fresh; trite, insipid*
n. **banality**
*Banal*, overused phrases and words are so numerous that it's hard to avoid them. Those of us who work on the *Times* cut these *banalities* from every article, including our own, because *banal* means boring, every time.

**TERSE** adj. *stripped of all but the essentials; concise or succinct, sometimes to the point of rudeness*
When you need encouragement, a *terse* response is disappointing. For instance, that small, *terse* "B" on my history paper seemed like a stingy answer to my weeks of research.

**RACONTEUR** n. *gifted talker or storyteller*
My English lit class read *The Importance of Being Earnest* by Oscar Wilde, a talented playwright, poet, and *raconteur* who, because he was so amusing, was an extremely popular guest. Wilde died in poverty in Paris; when a friend offered him champagne on his deathbed, Wilde remarked, "I am dying beyond my means."

**EUPHEMISM** n. *the use of a "nice" word or phrase instead of an offensive or terrible honest one; the word or phrase so used*
My last editorial was on the *euphemism* "ethnic cleansing," a phrase used to disguise the murders in Bosnia-Herzegovina and Rwanda. I enjoy some common *euphemisms*, such as "precocious" (spoiled brat) or "made redundant" ("fired" in Britain), but using a *euphemism* to cloak genocide is revolting.

---

**VOC/VOK = to call**

**vociferous**—*loudly, persistently vocal; clamorous*
    the *vociferous* wail of a hungry baby
    a *vociferous* message

**equivocal**—*open to two interpretations, evasive, unclear*
    a puzzling, *equivocal* answer
    an *equivocal*, uneasy reply

Also: **provoke, provocative, vocal, equivocate, evoke, evocative, invoke, invocation, revoke**

---

**SUCCINCT** adj. *brief, to the point; concise, pithy, terse*
Some critics favor the taut, *succinct* writing style of Hemingway or Cather. I enjoy a more colloquial style, like Mark Twain's in *Huckleberry Finn*. For the school paper, of course, we demand *succinct*, pithy articles.

**HACKNEYED** adj. *banal, overused, commonplace, trite*
The *hackney* was a breed of horse used to pull the old public coaches in England. From their regular, boring routine came the words *hackneyed* and *hack*.

**BOMBAST** n. *high-flown, pompous, "windbag" language*
The windy, *bombastic* mayor of our town likes to give speeches. Whenever he comes to school, this Bard of *Bombast* yaks away, one empty paragraph after another.

---

**LOC/LOQU/LOG/OLOGY = speech, study, word, talk**

**eloquent**—*extremely expressive (a gesture or words)*
    a moving, *eloquent* speech
    the *eloquent* bowing of his head

**loquacious**—*extremely talkative; gabby, garrulous*
    a *loquacious* parrot
    the *loquaciousness* born of loneliness

Also: **elocution, soliloquy, colloquial, prologue, epilogue, tautology** *(redundancy)*, **eulogy, psychology, biology**

---

**ARTICULATE** v. *to speak in a clear, effective way* adj. *clear and effective in manner;* also, *jointed or marked off (as "the beetle's articulated segments")*
Amy practices a lot, trying to *articulate* her lines perfectly. I admit that she's a really *articulate* performer, but life with an actress is hard to take.

**LACONIC** adj. *using as few words as possible; concise*
The old Greek Spartans from the area Laconia were big-deed-doers, not talkers, and came to be known as *laconic* folk. The most *laconic* communication I've heard was between Victor Hugo, author of *Les Miserables*, and his publisher. After the book came out, Hugo wrote: ? His publisher replied: !

**HYPERBOLE** n. *wild exaggeration, often on purpose for effect*
Reading Twain is fun, partly because he uses *hyperbole* so well. So does the cast on *Saturday Night Live*. The crazy exaggeration of *hyperbole* is probably as much fun for the actors as it is for their audience.

**LAMPOON** n. *verbal ridicule of a person; personal satire* v. *to ridicule*
The cast of *Saturday Night Live* loves to *lampoon* political figures, especially the president. They let their *lampooning* go as far as TV standards will allow.

**PLATITUDE** n. *a tired, trite old saying; a banality*
Remember our bombastic mayor? Well, one reason he's so boring is that he just mouths *platitudes*, like all windbags, and everybody's tired of hearing the same old sayings. *Platitudes* put people to sleep.

## MEMORY FIX

To learn these new words, write each one on a sheet of paper. Also write a synonym or definition for each and say the new words aloud as you work.

## TRUE OR FALSE

Read each sentence below to see how each word in this chapter is being used. Then mark **T** (true) or **F** (false) beside each.

1. You wouldn't enjoy a *raconteur* at your party. _____

2. We have many *euphemisms* for the word "died." _____

3. Hugh's repertoire of *hackneyed* jokes makes us roar with laughter. _____

4. A *laconic* speech is sure to drag on forever. _____

5. If I ask for a *terse* report, I mean a *succinct* one. _____

6. We sat spellbound and attentive as the speaker uttered one *platitude* after another. _____

7. *Hyperbole* is often used to good effect in a *lampoon*. _____

8. A person with a fine mind probably created this *banal* essay.

   _____

9. A pompous, self-important person is apt to deliver a *bombastic* speech. _____

10. The more *articulate* you are, the greater our chance of understanding your message. _____

## MATCHING
Match the words in column A with their meanings in column B.

|  | **A** | **B** |
|---|---|---|
| _____ | 1. eloquent | a. garrulous |
| _____ | 2. banality | b. great exaggeration |
| _____ | 3. vociferous | c. to say effectively |
| _____ | 4. trite | d. moving and expressive |
| _____ | 5. tautology | e. pompous |
| _____ | 6. articulate (v.) | f. evasive |
| _____ | 7. bombastic | g. platitude |
| _____ | 8. provoke | h. hackneyed |
| _____ | 9. loquacious | i. redundancy |

_____ 10. laconic            j. sparing of speech

_____ 11. hyperbole          k. to arouse or spark

_____ 12. equivocal          l. insistent and loud

## FILL IN THE BLANKS

From the words in this chapter, select the ones that best complete the meaning and logic of each sentence.

1. An editor who complains that your book lacks originality is saying that it is **t**_____ and **h**_____.

2. Five words that refer to the extremely economical use of language are **c**_____, **s**_____, **l**_____, **t**_____, and **p**_____.

3. "Mile-high pie" is an example of _____.

4. A **p**_____ is stale and overused, a trite remark, just like a **b**_____.

5. The opposite of a clearcut answer is a(n) _____ one.

**Answers for this chapter begin on page 197.**

# SYCOPHANTS HAVE BROWN NOSES

despot • sycophant • glutton • hedonist • hypocrite • heretic • charlatan • bigot • miser • insurgent • zealot • skeptic

**DESPOT** n. *a ruler with total control; a tyrant, autocrat*
Dude, my five-pound Yorky, sees himself as king of our house, a real *despot* with all of us under his paw. Amy's cat, Meatloaf, never yields to doggy *despotism*, of course.

**SYCOPHANT** n. *a brownnoser; one who flatters others; a toady*
Kids dislike *sycophants* because their brownnosing is so hypocritical. Powerful people must enjoy that servile flattery or we wouldn't have so many *sycophants*.

**GLUTTON** n. *one who is overly, almost sinfully, hungry for something, usually food* n. **glut** v. **to glut**
Amy's a *glutton* for roles on stage. "I'll play any part," she says. Recently, wrapped in thick padding, she portrayed *Gluttony* itself in a Christian morality play about the seven deadly sins.

**HEDONIST** n. *someone who lives for pleasure or happiness*
In class we discussed the Greek's doctrine of *hedonism*, which held that happiness or pleasure was the sole good in life. We contrasted the *hedonist's* pleasure-seeking goals with the Putitan's spiritual, work-oriented life, and ended up voting for a blend of the two—the old Greek "golden mean."

**HYPOCRITE** n. *one who pretends to a life or beliefs that he doesn't honestly have; a phony or fake*
The guys I know don't admire a *hypocrite* or *hypocrisy* of any kind. It's so phony. Think about tennis star Arthur Ashe, who was always honest and straightforward, never phony. "Not a *hypocritical* bone in him," my friend Jason says.

---

**ORA = to speak, pray**

inexorable—*not movable by any means; inflexible, relentless*
    *inexorable* hand of fate
    the *inexorable* march of time

oracle—*one who gives wise or especially meaningful advice*
    Greek *oracle* at Delphi
    the principal, our school's *oracle*

Also: **oracular, orator, peroration** *(a long, grandiose speech)*

---

**HERETIC** n. *one who differs from accepted belief or theory*
"Would you guys hang me as a *heretic* if I suggested eliminating the Social Corner?" I asked the newspaper staff. They agreed to cut the column and admitted that occasionally *heretics* have good ideas. (But often the mere suspicion of *heresy* is fatal. Witches were burned as *heretics* by fanatics, remember?)

**CHARLATAN** n. *a quack or fraud; a cheat, imposter*
My dad's office is just recovering from being cheated by a master *charlatan* who posed as a management consultant. The real skill of *charlatans* is lying, apparently.

**BIGOT** n. *one who stubbornly holds to his own opinions*
I hope age doesn't turn me into a narrow-minded *bigot* like some I know. I hate prejudice, and *bigoted* people are usually very opinionated.

---

**VER = truth**

verify—*to establish truth or accuracy; to confirm*
    *verify* his whereabouts
    try to *verify* his statement

aver—*to state firmly and convincingly; declare positively*
    "For all *averred*, I had killed the bird
    That made the breeze to blow.
    Ah wretch! said they, the bird to slay,
    That made the breeze to blow!"
    *The Rime of the Ancient Mariner*, Samuel Taylor Coleridge

Also: **verdict, verisimilitude, veracious** *(truthful)*

---

**MISER** n. *a greedy, grasping person (L.* miser = miserable*)*
One of my friends is really a *miser*, in contrast to the rest of us, who are
mainly generous guys. We tease him about being a *miserly* Scrooge type,
but his stinginess is less amusing as time goes by.

**INSURGENT** n. *a rebel; one who rises up in revolt*
As an editor I need to study newspapers, so I'm always aware of
*insurgent* forces in other countries. My sympathies are with *insurgents*
whenever they're revolting against a cruel political regime, as in Haiti.

**ZEALOT** n. *a fanatic; someone devoted beyond reason to a
cause or belief*
As the self-appointed defender of the family, Dude is our personal *zealot*.
Daily he patrols our property, barking *zealously*—fanatically—whenever
a stranger threatens to cross over into his territory.

**SKEPTIC** n. *one who doubts or waits to pass judgment*
Thomas Huxley, the famous English biologist, knew that a good scientist
was a *skeptic*. He said, "*Skepticism* is the highest of duties, blind faith the
one unpardonable sin." A *skeptic* is the opposite of a zealot or fanatic.

## MEMORY FIX
To learn these new words, write each one on a sheet of paper. Also write
a synonym or definition for each and say the words aloud as you work.

## FILL IN THE BLANKS
From the words in this chapter, select the one that best completes the
meaning and logic of each phrase. Note which tense or form of the word
is required for sense.

1. dangerous crew of armed _____ spearheading
   the revolt

2. the _____ habit of saying one thing while
   thinking another

3. needs one _____ week just having fun this
   summer

4. a true workaholic, a regular _____ for more
   challenges

5. as _____ as the cycle of the seasons

6. those practiced _____ who skillfully deceive us

7. looked like a real diamond, but I was still _____

8. a strong autocrat, but even so a benevolent

_____

9. the _____ in our midst, determined to go against established tradition

10. suffering from an excess of zeal, a _____ for sure

11. hoarding his candy like a _____ hoards his wealth

12. the most _____, prejudiced person I ever met

13. the servile behavior of a known _____

14. necessary that you _____ the accuracy of this report

## RHYME TIME

Complete these couplets of pretty awful poetry (PAP) with the correct form of one of this chapter's new words **or** an important synonym.

1. Said Orson Welles, whose size doubled by twice,
   "_____ is not a secret vice."

2. We keep loony Aunt Tilly up in the attic,
   'Cause everyone knows she's a raving _____.

3. When I need advice on a matter historical,
   I ask my teacher, the school's living _____.

4. A _____ says, "I was born to doubt,
   Until the facts of the matter come out."

5. We couldn't believe he gave her that plant,
   But he's a toady, you know, a _____.

6. "Lookin' for fun in all the right places,"
   Sings the _____ eager for bright party faces.

7. Nature's _____ laws we spurn,
   Only if we're too dimwitted to learn.

8. I was quick to _____ when I testified,
   That Hugo would never run off or hide.

## MATCHING

In column B, find two synonyms or phrases to explain each word in column A, and write their letters on the correct lines.

| | A | B | |
|---|---|---|---|
| _____ | 1. miser | a. bias | i. fake, fraud |
| _____ | 2. heretic | b. corroborate | j. one in revolt |
| _____ | 3. despot | c. hoarder | k. prejudice |
| _____ | 4. charlatan | d. nonbeliever | l. fanatical |
| _____ | 5. bigotry | e. rebel | m. Scrooge |
| _____ | 6. verify | f. tyrant | n. overeager |
| _____ | 7. zealous | g. imposter | o. confirm |
| _____ | 8. insurgent | h. autocrat | p. one who differs |

**Answers for this chapter begin on page 198.**

# HOW GERMANE, MY DEAR

---

**fervent • germane • fortuitous • grueling • indulgent • vulnerable • profuse • superficial • uniform • listless • incessant • unobtrusive**

---

**FERVENT** adj. *full of strong emotion; impassioned*
Meatloaf vents her anger in *fervent* yowls when another cat invades our yard. The *fervor* of Meatloaf's response to feline trespassers seems much louder at night, when we *fervently* wish she'd shut up.

**GERMANE** adj. *fitting and appropriate; relevant; pertinent*
The Mark Twain quotes I like best aren't *germane* to my talk, so I can't use them. Our speech teacher always says, "Omit the extras and concentrate on the *germane* material when giving a brief talk."

**FORTUITOUS** adj. *happening by chance; accidental*
Meatloaf stalks mice deliberately, but she also has her share of *fortuitous* meetings. Happening upon a mouse is *fortuitous* not only for Meatloaf but also for the mouse, who would never have planned to meet a cat.

**GRUELING** adj. *demanding and exhausting; punishing, tiring*
In one *grueling* day, the newspaper staff washed over 400 cars to raise money for a new computer. At home later, exhausted but proud, I told the folks just how *grueling* a task it had been.

**INDULGENT** adj. *generous to a fault; lenient, not critical*
We've been too *indulgent* with Dude, and so he's badly spoiled. We've agreed to stop *indulging* him right now. As Shakespeare warned us, an *indulgent* person loves "not wisely but too well."

**VULNERABLE** adj. *open to physical or mental damage or hurt*
Unaware of the word *vulnerable* as a kid, I still knew the feeling of being open to attack from mean guys on the playground at recess. When you're *vulnerable*, you know you're without a good defense.

---

**CLAUS/CLUD/CLUS = close, shut**

**preclude**—*to forestall, hinder, avert, or prevent*
the storm *precluded* our hike
that rule *precludes* his joining

**recluse**—*a hermit; one living a solitary life*
a wealthy, eccentric *recluse*
his withdrawn, *reclusive* life

Also: **exclude, exclusion, claustrophobia, include, inclusion**

---

**PROFUSE** adj. *in great abundance; bountiful; lavish; lush*
The phrase *"profuse* apologies" describes a gushing flood of "I'm sorrys." During a tough wrestling match, my *profuse* perspiration is another kind of flood. Unfortunately, our county has a *profusion* of great high school wrestlers.

**SUPERFICIAL** adj. *on the surface, shallow; not deep, serious, or important; cursory, not thorough*
I got some *superficial* cuts from cleats in the last soccer game; fortunately, *superficial* wounds normally heal without causing trouble. In contrast, a *superficial* judgment is apt to cause lots of trouble.

**UNIFORM** adj. *consistent (as opposed to varied); the same*
I think *uniformity* of design, as in a row of identical houses or apartments, is boring. But at school I want consistency and fairness—*uniform* attendance policies and *uniform* grading systems.

---

**POT/POSS = to be powerful or able**

**potent**—*powerful; effective or efficacious*
a *potent* remedy
a *potent* idea
an Eastern *potentate* (ruler)

**omnipotent**—*all-powerful*
*omnipotent* ruler
the old Greek *omnipotent* gods

Also: **potential, possible, possess**

---

**LISTLESS** adj. *lacking energy or enthusiasm; indifferent or languid; uncaring*

When we found Meatloaf staring at her food with dull, *listless* eyes, we knew she was sick. Any *listlessness* toward dinner on that cat's part is serious. When I had the flu, I remember feeling *listless* toward everything.

**INCESSANT** adj. *going on without interruption; unceasing; continuous*

En route to the vet's office, Meatloaf's *incessant* yowling drove us bats. Like many cats in a car, she cries continuously and pitifully—an *incessant* reminder that she never asked to go for a ride.

**UNOBTRUSIVE** adj. *not noticeable; inconspicuous; or, not aggressive*

Our pets Dude and Meatloaf don't know the word *unobtrusive*. Meatloaf thinks, why utter a dainty, *unobtrusive* mew when you can yowl? And Dude has spent his entire aggressive life seeking fights instead of being *unobtrusive*.

## MEMORY FIX

To learn these new words, write each one on a sheet of paper. Also write a synonym or definition for each and say the words aloud as you work.

## FILL IN THE BLANKS

To complete each sentence, select the correct **noun form** (as shown below) of the adjectives in this chapter's list.

| | | | |
|---|---|---|---|
| fervor | indulgence | listlessness | profusion |
| uniformity | superficiality | vulnerability | unobtrusiveness |

1.  I object to the _____ of this assessment, especially since I had requested an in-depth evaluation.

2.  By the end of our vacation, I had relaxed to the point of almost total _____ !

3.  We were excited by the _____ of the cheering crowd that lined the marathon runners' path.

4. In Glacier National Park in late June, the wildflowers erupt on the hills and roadsides in brilliant _____.

5. Realizing the _____ of animals on our planet, concerned people have organized to protect these dependent creatures.

6. "I'm begging your _____ for a minute," the speaker said, "while I digress briefly."

7. From a human's viewpoint, the owl that sleeps by day and hunts silently by night is a model of _____.

8. When we bake chocolate chip cookies, we try for _____ so that all of them have the same amount of chocolate.

## TRUE OR FALSE

Read each sentence below to see if the words in this chapter are being used properly. Then mark **T** (true) or **F** (false) beside each sentence.

1. If you've never really worked out at a health spa, the first experience is fun but a trifle *grueling*. _____

2. The painful twinges of out-of-shape muscles would be more acceptable if they were *incessant*. _____

3. His fondness for good company is only natural in a confirmed *recluse*. _____

4. Because his diving is still weak after years of practice, I think his *potential* is limited in that sport. _____

5. When a highway becomes treacherous, officials often *preclude* travel until conditions improve. _____

**6.** A pertinent anecdote is one that is *germane* to the topic.

_____

**7.** The girl's *fervent* plea to the vet to save her beloved pet raccoon moved us to tears. _____

**8.** A planned, organized meeting cannot be termed *fortuitous*.

_____

**9.** Erratic guidelines are more helpful than *uniform* ones. _____

**10.** An *unobtrusive* tooth fairy is the most successful. _____

## MATCHING ANTONYMS

Knowing opposites is helpful. Match the words on the left by writing the letters of two antonyms on the correct lines.

| | | | |
|---|---|---|---|
| _____ | 1. germane | a. irrelevant | k. restful |
| _____ | 2. profuse | b. weak | l. deeply serious |
| _____ | 3. uniform | c. aggressive | m. inappropriate |
| _____ | 4. grueling | d. restrained | n. stingy |
| _____ | 5. superficial | e. inconsistent | o. unforgiving |
| _____ | 6. potent | f. exhilarating | p. varied |
| _____ | 7. indulgent | g. thorough | q. ineffective |
| _____ | 8. listless | h. bouncy | r. friendly |
| _____ | 9. reclusive | i. gregarious | s. enthusiastic |
| _____ | 10. unobtrusive | j. critical | t. conspicuous |

**Answers for this chapter begin on page 198.**

---

arrogant • disdain • fastidious • haughty • disparage • deprecate • condescend • supercilious • contempt • pretentious • scoff • complacent

---

**ARROGANT** adj. *proud, overbearing; snootily self-important*
Despite his office, President Abraham Lincoln was never *arrogant*, but humble instead. A much later president, John F. Kennedy, said, "When power leads man toward *arrogance*, poetry reminds him of his limitations."

**DISDAIN** n. *scorn; snooty disapproval or dislike; contempt* v. **to disdain** adj. **disdainful**
No animal can show *disdain* as well as a cat. If Meatloaf's food is not quite right, she *disdains* to eat it and scratches around the bowl as if to bury the offending meal.

**FASTIDIOUS** adj. *extremely fussy and particular; meticulous*
A healthy cat is *fastidious* about its appearance and grooms its fur meticulously. A sick cat abandons this natural *fastidiousness*.

**HAUGHTY** adj. *openly and disdainfully proud; snooty* n.
**hauteur, haughtiness**
You've heard that pride goes before a fall, but the old Biblical proverb actually says, "Pride goeth before destruction and a *haughty* spirit before a fall." You've seen *haughtiness*, that "I'm above you" attitude, right?

**DISPARAGE** v. *to belittle or downgrade (someone or something); to decry, depreciate, minimize*
When I was a kid, a bigger neighbor boy regularly *disparaged* my homemade tree house. I remember how that *disparagement* hurt and how it reduced my pride in my creation.

---

**ROG = to ask**

derogatory—*scornful, disparaging, downgrading, belittling*
of a *derogatory* nature
a highly *derogatory* critique

prerogative—*a special right or privilege*
a ruler's *prerogative*
her natural *prerogative* as the oldest

Also: **interrogate, arrogant, abrogate, surrogate**

---

**DEPRECATE** v. *to disapprove mildly, with regret* adj.
**deprecatory**, *hoping to avoid disapproval*
It's clear that Mom *deprecates* the mess in my room, but she understands that it's my space. When relatives are critical, Mom defends me with a *deprecatory* shrug and a smile.

**CONDESCEND** v. *to come down in level, unbend, stoop*
Meatloaf *condescends* to play hide-and-seek with Dude if she thinks no one will see her being kittenish again. Likewise, my serious, formal grandfather will now and then *condescend* to listen to my rock music.

**SUPERCILIOUS** adj. *excessively proud; disdainfully superior*
Explaining her role in our school play, Amy said, "I'm playing an insufferably snooty lady, someone totally *supercilious*. I'm supposed to reek of *superciliousness* in every speech.

---

**RID/RIS = to laugh**

deride—*to mock or make fun of; to ridicule*
don't *deride* his shyness
humbled by his *derision*

risible—*laughable, funny; used for laughter*
a truly *risible* situation
*risible* facial muscles

Also: **ridicule, ridiculous, risibility, derisive, derisory**

---

**CONTEMPT** n. *total lack of respect; disdain; scorn*
Our English class wrote essays on this Schopenhauer quote: "Hatred comes from the heart; *contempt* from the head; and neither feeling is quite within our control." That's probably true, but we can use *contempt* for good purposes, such as being openly *contemptuous* of those who damage our planet.

**PRETENTIOUS** adj. *showy, self-important, pompous; insisting on recognition, often unjustifiably*
The newly rich (nouveau riche, to my French teacher) often live in *pretentious* houses and drive expensive cars. *Pretentiousness* says, "Look at me. I'm important."

**SCOFF** v. *to make fun of, mock; to belittle by jeering or contemptuous talk*
A few times we *scoffed* at guys who got pinned in the first period of their wrestling matches, but the coach stopped that. "Come out to support each other, not to *scoff*," he ordered.

**COMPLACENT** adj. *self-satisfied, smug*
Dude quivers all over with *complacency* after chasing off an intruder. As he returns to his position on our porch, he twitches his topknot *complacently*—smug in the knowledge that he's done his duty.

## MEMORY FIX
To learn these new words, write each one on a sheet of paper. Also write a synonym or definition for each and say the words aloud as you work.

## MATCHING
Circle the two words or phrases that best explain the meaning of each of the words in bold type.

1. **fastidious**
   (A) swift
   (B) exceedingly particular
   (C) meticulous
   (D) unpleasant

2. **deprecate**
   (A) reduce
   (B) deny
   (C) disapprove of
   (D) regret

3. **arrogant**
   (A) prideful
   (B) questioning
   (C) thoughtless
   (D) overbearing

4. **condescend**
   (A) stoop
   (B) unbend
   (C) forgive
   (D) offend

**5. contempt**
   (A) timely assistance
   (B) scorn
   (C) disdain
   (D) refusal

**6. scoff**
   (A) torture
   (B) critique
   (C) belittle
   (D) mock or jeer

**7. complacent**
   (A) smug
   (B) self-satisfied
   (C) peaceful
   (D) well-located

**8. prerogative**
   (A) annoyance
   (B) privilege
   (C) position
   (D) right

**9. deride**
   (A) scoff at
   (B) dismount
   (C) ridicule
   (D) hoard

**10. disparage**
   (A) resist
   (B) minimize
   (C) decry
   (D) avoid

## WORDS IN CONTEXT

Write the meaning of each italicized word on the lines provided.

**1.** back stiffly erect, nose *haughtily* in the air

_____

**2.** filling an otherwise empty life with *pretentious* objects

_____

**3.** raised a *supercilious* eyebrow and gave a loud "Humph!"

_____

**4.** viewing the culprit with a look of utter *disdain*

_____

**5.** gentle cleric who *disdained* pulp literature

_____

**6.** cringing as he read the *derogatory* review

_____

7. insulted by their *condescending* manner

_____

8. enjoying my *prerogative* as the leader

_____

9. bowing her head in a *self-deprecatory* way

_____

10. regarding my handiwork with a certain *complacence*

_____

## ANALOGIES

Circle the one word pair in each list below that expresses the same relationship as the pair in capital letters.

1. **NAPOLEON : ARROGANCE**
   (A) Ben Franklin : hedonism
   (B) Hitler : fastidiousness
   (C) Tchaikovsky : bombast
   (D) Twain : satire
   (E) Maya Angelou : journalism

2. **REMARK : DISPARAGING**
   (A) appearance : unobtrusive
   (B) attitude : scoffing
   (C) speech : articulate
   (D) article : meticulous
   (E) design : risible

3. **PRIDE : HAUTEUR**
   (A) pretentiousness : wealth
   (B) disdain : disgust
   (C) sorrow : contempt
   (D) satisfaction : complacency
   (E) youth : vulnerability

4. **DERISION : RIDICULE**
   (A) sweetness : indulgence
   (B) disdain : honor
   (C) prerogative : duty
   (D) seclusion : profusion
   (E) scorn : contempt

**Answers for this chapter begin on page 198.**

# LISTS 1-5 REVIEW

Here's one more chance to practice using the words in lists
1 to 5. But first, read each list and say each word
and its meaning out loud. Over one third of
us learn best through our EARS.

## FIND THE ODDBALL

In each word group, cross out the oddball—the one *unrelated* word or
phrase.

1. bigot   phony   hypocrite   heretic   fake

2. ridicule   derision   hauteur   disdain   derogation

3. insist   assent   comply   yield   acquiesce

4. clamorous   noisy   vociferous   persistently vocal   nasty

5. articulate   hyperbole   lucid   effective   clear

6. relevant   pertinent   germane   interesting   related to

7. provoke   preclude   forestall   hinder   prevent

8. proud   inevitable   arrogant   haughty   supercilious

9. flatterer   toady   sycophant   brownnoser   hedonist

10. hackneyed   terse   clipped   concise   succinct

## TRUE OR FALSE

Check these sentences for correctness. Then mark **T** (true) or **F** (false) beside each.

1. *Euphemisms* allow you to say in public what would otherwise be unacceptable or possibly even cruel. _____

2. *Hackneyed* phrases, such as "he eats like a horse" or "she's thin as a rail," are not examples of *hyperbole*. _____

3. You should avoid hiring speakers who are very *eloquent*. _____

4. You shouldn't *verify* data for a research paper. _____

5. *Hedonists* are careful to avoid parties. _____

6. A *miser* enjoys supporting several charities. _____

7. *Zealots*, or *fanatics*, rarely *condone* ideologies that run counter to theirs and may even *disparage* contrasting views in a most *articulate* manner. _____

8. In *My Family and Other Animals*, Gerald Durrell pokes fun at everyone in his family, making a book-length *lampoon*. _____

9. As an ancient Greek general, you might wish to consult the famous *oracle* at Delphi before a battle. _____

10. If you prefer short meetings, select *loquacious* board members, not *laconic* ones. _____

# FIND THE SYNONYM

From the choices offered, select the missing synonym for each numbered word group and write that synonym on the corresponding line.

| | | | |
|---|---|---|---|
| to concur | to condone | charlatan | profuse |
| precursor | banal | inexorable | listless |
| to chastise | equivocal | grueling | potent |

1. unclear   evasive   confusing   undecided

   _____

2. to agree   coincide   assent   approve _____

3. trite   hackneyed   commonplace   stale

   _____

4. languid   indifferent   uncaring _____

5. to scold   castigate   punish   censure _____

6. impostor   quack   fraud   cheat _____

7. to overlook   excuse   pardon _____

8. forerunner   harbinger   herald _____

9. immovable   relentless   inflexible _____

10. punishing   tiring   demanding   exhausting

    _____

11. abundant   bountiful   lavish   lush _____

12. powerful   effective   efficacious _____

# WHO SAID THAT?

From the choices offered, write the *type of speaker* for each of the following comments.

| | | | |
|---|---|---|---|
| raconteur | glutton | skeptic | interrogator |
| equivocator | heretic | recluse | orator |
| despot | insurgent | scoffer | deprecator |

1. "Friends, Romans, countrymen, lend me your ears."

   _____

2. Did I tell you the one about Anansi the Spider and his cousin . . .? _____

3. Could I have another steak? _____

4. It's peaceful here alone on the island. _____

5. Are you sure? Did you run tests that prove your ideas are actual facts? _____

6. Clean your room now or else! _____

7. Gee, there's nothing like a good uprising. _____

8. That's nothing. I was riding a bike at age three.

   _____

9. I don't believe that anymore; I can't. _____

10. Well, maybe and maybe not. It sort of seems that way, and then again it doesn't. _____

11. I repeat. Is that your toad in the soup? _____

12. I didn't really mean to, she said, shrugging.

    _____

## MATCHING

Match the words in column A with their meanings in column B and then write the meanings in the space provided.

|  |  | A | B |
| --- | --- | --- | --- |
| _____ |  | 1. coalesce | pompous language |
| _____ |  | 2. laud | accidental |
| _____ |  | 3. cursory | to ridicule |
| _____ |  | 4. bombast | disdain, scorn |
| _____ |  | 5. platitude | to scatter or fan out |
| _____ |  | 6. aver | to obliterate; wear away |
| _____ |  | 7. fortuitous | lenient |
| _____ |  | 8. deride | continuous |
| _____ |  | 9. prerogative | to praise |
| _____ |  | 10. contempt | superficial or hasty |
| _____ |  | 11. augment | to come together |
| _____ |  | 12. disperse | to declare firmly |
| _____ |  | 13. efface | banality |
| _____ |  | 14. indulgent | to increase |
| _____ |  | 15. incessant | right or privilege |

**Answers for this review lesson begin on page 199.**

# VERBS TO HEED

---

**garner • mar • heed • meander • nullify • obliterate • mitigate • obscure • peruse • raze • placate • rebuff**

---

**GARNER** v. *to gather or collect; accumulate; earn*
Our paper's sports editor *garners* all the information he can about an opponent before a crucial game. He says, "I go to their practices with the goal of *garnering* any clue, however small, that will help us to compete better."

**MAR** v. *to spoil or damage; to injure or blemish*
We all hate having something nice *marred*. For instance, a zit really *mars* a kid's appearance. When flying gravel *marred* the paint on Dad's new car, he went ballistic.

**HEED** v. *to listen to, pay attention to, consider; to mind*
Meatloaf *heeds* our orders only if she feels like it. Deep in a cat's soul must be the motto: To *Heed* is To Yield Independence. One day, *heedless* of our pleading, Meatloaf made her way to the top of the neighbor's giant oak.

**MEANDER** v. *to wander casually with no set plan; to ramble*
A speech should not *meander* but should follow a clear outline; nor should an airplane *meander* through the skies. But I'm glad that streams and creeks *meander* in no set pattern across the countryside.

**NULLIFY** v. *to render unimportant or without worth; to negate or invalidate; to annul legally*
The Student Council voted to *nullify* some regulations passed by former councils. We made them "*null* and void," as the expression goes.

**OBLITERATE** v. *to erase completely, wiping out all traces*
A group of us watched from a high dune as the tide came in and *obliterated* our sand castles, leaving the shore flat and smooth. I wish I could *obliterate* as completely those old, childish nightmares.

---

**MUT/MUTAT = to change**

**immutable**—*changeless and unchanging; unalterable, eternal*
Nature's *immutable* laws
the *immutable* power of love

**mutation**—*significant genetic change; the one changed*
a *mutation* in the human form that evolved over time
scientifically engineered *mutations* in corn plants

Also: **mutable, mutant, commute, permutation, transmutation**

---

**MITIGATE** v. *to ease, making less severe; to alleviate or relieve*
We slathered antihistamine cream on Amy's bee stings, hoping to *mitigate* the pain. She said that the burning and itching were somewhat *mitigated* but certainly not obliterated.

**OBSCURE** v. *to make dim or unclear; to conceal, hide* adj.
**obscure**, *vague, mysterious, remote, dark*
As a wrestler, I like to *obscure* the real objective of my movements and catch an opponent off guard. Chess and checkers players *obscure* their strategies, too, I'm sure.

**PERUSE** v. *to study or examine carefully* n. **perusal**
The guidance counselors urged us to *peruse* the booklet *Taking the SAT*. Also, they suggested we *peruse* a self-help book that explains each kind of problem. After a *perusal* of *SAT Success*, I decided I needed to brush up on geometry.

---

**PON/POS = to place or put**

**posit**—*to suppose, propose, suggest; to assume or affirm*
let's *posit* this theory
when he first *posited* that idea

**proponent**—*one who talks in favor of something, an advocate*
a famous *proponent* of exercise
hardly a *proponent* of sloth

Also: **position, postpone, component, exponent, repository, expose, depose, transpose, deposit, dispose, juxtapose**

---

**RAZE** v. *to tear down completely, to demolish*
We spent last weekend *razing* the old barn on our property. We'd hoped to save it, but since it was too decrepit to restore, we were forced to *raze* it instead.

**PLACATE** v. *to calm, soothe, or appease, especially by offering to "be nice" or to do someone a favor*
Last year's seniors were a crazy bunch, always in trouble and trying to *placate* the principal for what they'd done. As time weny by, she said she couldn't be *placated* any longer.

**REBUFF** v. *to criticize harshly or to reject someone, often by snubbing them (ignoring them)*
Meatloaf *rebuffed* Dude's offers of puppy friendship when he first joined our family. Do you think a dog feels hurt the way a human does when he suffers a *rebuff?* Dude didn't allow himself to be *rebuffed* for long, of course.

## MEMORY FIX
To learn these new words, write each one on a sheet of paper. Also write a synonym or definition for each and say the words aloud as you work.

## RHYME TIME
Complete these couplets of pretty awful poetry with the correct form of one of the new words in this chapter.

1. An unusual word that at first makes us frown,
   To _____ a building means to tear it down!

2. Something _____ forever stays the same,
   Unlike that fleeting idol called fame.

3. The detective announced, "A theory I'll _____.
   The criminal's hiding right here in this closet."

4. Down fragrant paths of rose and oleander,
   My love and I were happy to _____.
   (Oh, brother.)

5. A _____ is a really odd star for a show,
   But remember those Ninja turtles we know?

## MATCHING
Circle the two words or phrases that best explain the meaning of each of the words in bold type.

1. **mar**
   (A) blemish
   (B) confuse
   (C) spoil
   (D) annoy

2. **mitigate**
   (A) discuss
   (B) adjust
   (C) relieve
   (D) alleviate

3. **obliterate**
   (A) disguise
   (B) efface
   (C) wipe out
   (D) cover up

4. **rebuff**
   (A) snub
   (B) restore
   (C) polish
   (D) reject

5. **garner**
   (A) avoid
   (B) collect
   (C) strew around
   (D) accumulate

6. **obscure**
   (A) cloud over
   (B) conceal
   (C) caution
   (D) negate

7. **peruse**
   (A) scan
   (B) memorize
   (C) study carefully
   (D) examine

8. **meander**
   (A) walk
   (B) wander
   (C) ramble
   (D) flirt

9. **placate**
   (A) enjoy
   (B) entertain
   (C) soothe
   (D) appease

10. **raze**
    (A) lift up
    (B) tear down
    (C) devour
    (D) demolish

11. **nullify**
    (A) invalidate
    (B) join legally
    (C) end
    (D) negate

12. **heed**
    (A) wait on
    (B) mind or obey
    (C) consider
    (D) learn

## SUBSTITUTION

Replace each italicized word or phrase with the correct word from the
word list in this unit, including words from roots.

1. I refuse to *pay attention to* that wacko advice!

   _____

2. She's always been a *person in favor* of recycling. _____

3. That splash of aftershave certainly *spoiled* the tabletop.

   _____

4. The digressive nature of his lecture unfortunately *made dim,
   mysterious, and unclear* his major points. _____

5. Her explanation should *soothe and relieve* Claire's anger.

   _____

6. Queen Elizabeth I *firmly rejected* those who even hinted that the
   English Navy might lose to the Spanish Armada.

   _____

7. We were finally able to *make promises of never doing that
   again* Mom and Dad, but it wasn't easy. _____

8. I spent hours *studying carefully* the driver's manual before I took
   the test. _____

9. As long as they adhere to the Constitution, members of the
   Supreme Court may *render null and void* a decision by a lower
   court. _____

10. At summer meets with neighboring towns, Amy has *collected*
    several awards for backstroke and freestyle swimming.

    _____

**Answers for this chapter begin on page 200.**

# BEWARE A PARSIMONIOUS PREDECESSOR

---

**virtuoso • termerity • volition • torpor • quandary • trepidation • zenith • reticence • respite • parsimony • nostalgia • predecessor**

---

**VIRTUOSO** n. *a highly skilled performer*
As Meatloaf yowled eloquently from the top of the oak tree, Dad observed, "Hmm, we have a true feline *virtuoso*. Now if only she were a *virtuoso* at climbing, she could get herself down from there."

**TEMERITY** n. *unwise boldness; rash or reckless behavior*
Meatloaf showed unusual *temerity* in scaling that oak. Dude, of course, is forever hurtling into danger with a *temerity* that would never occur to a more sensible dog.

**VOLITION** n. *use of your own will, by your choice*
Animals were once viewed as beings of instinct only, with no powers of *volition*. Now we know that animals act on their own *volition* fairly often.

**TORPOR** n. *sluggishness, lethargy; inability to think or act quickly* adj. **torpid**
To be absolutely pooped is to feel *torpor*. I was in a totally *torpid* state once after a grueling wrestling match. Boxers must feel a similar *torpor* after their matches.

**QUANDARY** n. *a feeling a puzzlement or doubt*
Choosing a college is a perplexing process that has most of us in a state of *quandary*. It's a *quandary* that will remain, I think, until the final decision is made.

**TREPIDATION** n. *fear, worry, apprehension*
I keep seeing the phrase "in fear and *trepidation*," which seems repetitious, because *trepidation* often means fear. I'd rather say, "He went forward timidly, with *trepidation*."

---

**ARCH = chief or main; ruler**

**hierarchy**—*a series arranged by rank or grade*
>   at the top of the *hierarchy*
>   her place in the *hierarchy*

**anarchy**—*lack of government, often resulting in lawlessness*
>   historical *anarchy* in the Balkans
>   *anarchy* in the ranks

Also: **patriarch, matriarch, monarch, archangel, architect**

---

**ZENITH** n. *the highest point, or acme; point of culmination*
Although *zenith* means the highest point in the sky above us, I more often hear it used in phrases like "when his powers were at their *zenith*" or "at the *zenith* of her career."

**RETICENCE** n. *quietness and restraint in personality* adj.
**reticent,** *silent, restrained, reserved*
President Calvin Coolidge, a silent, restrained New Englander, was famous for his *reticence*. On hearing that this most *reticent* of men had died, writer Dorothy Parker said, "How can you tell?"

**RESPITE** n. *time of relief from activity; rest, pause, lull*
Thanksgiving weekend came as a welcome *respite* after a crazy autumn. That's the purpose of a vacation, of course—to act as a *respite* from our normal, busy lives.

---

**LU/LUC = light**

**lucid**—*clear and distinct; sensible, intelligible*
>   a graceful, *lucid* talk
>   having recovered *lucid* speech

**elucidate**—*to explain fully and clearly*
>   *elucidate* his problem, please
>   always happy to *elucidate*

Also: **lucidity, translucent, luminous, Lucifer, lucubration**

---

**PARSIMONY** n. *extreme stinginess; thrift; penny-pinching*
As all of Dickens's readers know, the character Ebenezer Scrooge is synonymous with *parsimony*. Underpaying his staff and failing to heat his business office were only a few of Scrooge's *parsimonious* habits.

**NOSTALGIA** n. *a sentimental longing for a past time or state*
adj. **nostalgic**
My grandparents are a typically *nostalgic* pair who always tell the same stories about my dad as a kid. *Nostalgia* for the past and the way things were must be a natural part of growing older.

**PREDECESSOR** n. *an ancestor; prior person in a position*
My *predecessor* on the newspaper was an editor who turned the various staff members into a close family of coworkers. My grandparents, who are my hereditary *predecessors* and who aren't one bit parsimonious, generously provide a vacation spot for our entire family each summer.

## MEMORY FIX
To learn these new words, write each one on a sheet of paper. Also write a synonym or definition for each and say the words aloud as you work.

## FILL IN THE BLANKS
From the new words in this chapter, select the one that best completes the meaning and logic of each sentence. Note which tense or form of the word is required for sense.

1. Meadowlark Lemon, a magician on the basketball court, and Itzhak Perlman, a gifted violinist, are both _____ in their respective fields.

2. The alternatives were so different and so complex that I was left in a complete _____.

3. When the anaesthetic has worn off and the patient is _____, the newspaper reporter will want to interview him.

4. A _____ man, Jacob Grunch amassed a fortune through careful management and total disregard of others' needs.

5. I wouldn't mind crossing the desert at night, but never when the sun is at its _____!

6. _____ in every limb of his body, the hibernating bear stretched slowly, then settled back into sleep.

7. I remember my summers at camp with _____, sorry that I'm too old to return.

8. Before the principal called him to her office, my friend Greg went of his own _____, hoping to mitigate her anger by his voluntary appearance.

9. Today's politicians don't dare be _____ folk, because the TV era demands articulate speakers.

10. We're amazed every year at the _____ of the squirrels who collect acorns from our porch, despite the vigilance of Meatloaf and Dude.

## MATCHING ANTONYMS

Knowing opposites is helpful. Match the words on the left with their opposites on the right.

| | | |
|---|---|---|
| _____ | 1. trepidation* | to obscure |
| _____ | 2. reticence | descendant |
| _____ | 3. zenith | hyperactive |
| _____ | 4. torpid | order |
| _____ | 5. temerity | confidence |
| _____ | 6. elucidate | beginner |
| _____ | 7. anarchy | generosity |
| _____ | 8. virtuoso | nadir (lowest point) |
| _____ | 9. predecessor | bombast |
| _____ | 10. parsimony | timidity |

*Knowing what trepidation is, what does *intrepid* probably mean?
_____

## FIND THE ODDBALL

In each word group below, cross out the oddball, the one unrelated word or phrase.

**1.** ranking   hierarchy   assortment   series

**2.** break   angle   rest   lull   respite

**3.** niece   ancestor   grandparent   predecessor

**4.** instinct   will   volition   desire

**5.** apprehension   worry   temperament   trepidation

**6.** quest   preplexity   quandary   puzzlement

**7.** betrayal   stinginess   miserliness   parsimony

**8.** transparent   coherent   intelligible   lucid

**9.** rashness   fear   boldness   temerity

**10.** quaintness   restraint   silence   reticence

**Answers for this chapter begin on page 200.**

# THAT'S ME!

---

**astute • discerning • formidable • indefatigable • sage • profound • judicious • meticulous • painstaking • resilient • tenacious • benevolent**

---

**ASTUTE** adj. *wise, shrewd, perceptive; perspicacious*
Like everyone in my class, I hope to make a fairly *astute* college selection. Luckily, our guidance counselors are pros and have made several *astute* suggestions that will help me to narrow my choices.

**DISCERNING** adj. *showing wisdom and wise judgment; discriminating wisely among choices* v. **to discern** n. **discernment**
Emily Dickinson wrote, "Much Madness is divinest Sense—To a *discerning* eye." My class wrote short essays on that couplet, trying to *discern* its meaning. We're gradually becoming *discerning* readers and interpreters of poetry.

**FORMIDABLE** adj. *fostering respect or awe; arousing fear; redoubtable*
Because the opponents I'd normally face in our next wrestling meet are *formidable* beyond belief, I have to sweat down to the next lowest weight class in order to wrestle competitively. Of course, nothing helps a guy sweat like the fear of a *formidable* adversary!

**INDEFATIGABLE** adj. *untiring, tireless (see root of "fatigue")*
Mom's *indefatigable* determination to learn computer programming is amazing. Our whole family is stubborn, though, so the word *indefatigable* often applies to us.

**SAGE** adj. *wise as a result of experience and thought; shrewd and discerning of judgment; prudent* adj. **sagacious**, *shrewd* n. **sage**, *wise elder*
Look at all the meaning *sage* conveys in only four letters. Perhaps author Ernest Hemingway made a very *sage* decision by using mostly short, punchy words.

---

**LEV = light (as in weight), to raise**

**leverage**—*a form of control, power, or effectiveness; referring to the use of a lever*
 used his position as *leverage* in the takeover

**alleviate**—*to lessen or relieve the severity of a condition*
 *alleviate* his pain
 hoping to *alleviate* their sorrow

Also: **elevate, levitate, elevator, lever, levee, levity**

---

**PROFOUND** adj. *intellectually deep; deeply important; complete or all-encompassing*
Our new principal is a *profoundly* thoughtful man, given to uttering *profound* thoughts whenever they occur to him. This talkativeness is a *profound* change from his predecessor, who was extremely reticent.

**JUDICIOUS** adj. *showing good judgment; wise, discreet*
I always think of *judge*, *justice*, and *jury* when I see the root *ju*, an old root of Jove and Zeus that actually means "shining sky." Of course, gods have always been thought to live in the sky and to be the most *judicious* of beings.

**METICULOUS** adj. *particular down to the tiniest detail*
Meatloaf is a *meticulous* groomer. This care results in a glossy fur coat that advertises her *meticulous* nature.

---

**TEN/TENT/TIN/TAIN = to hold, contain**

**tenet**—*a major belief, principle, or doctrine of a group*
 a main *tenet* of Judaism
 one *tenet* of that profession

**untenable**—*indefensible; unable to be occupied (by a tenant)*
 a wholly *untenable* theory
 a rundown, *untenable* building

Also: **tenant, tenure, content, contention, detain, detention, contain, abstain, abstinence, sustain, sustenance**

---

**PAINSTAKING** adj. *revealing much care and effort*
With *painstaking* care, I restored the used car that I inherited on my eighteenth birthday. In the true sense of the word *painstaking*, I took great pains to wash, paint, and wax every inch of this incredible treasure.

**RESILIENT** adj. *elastic; able to "snap back" after change or misfortune* n. **resilience**
Dude's personality is *resilient*; he bounces back to his cheerful, optimistic self within minutes of being scolded. Without this natural *resilience*, he'd be sorrowful much of the time, because he gets frequently corrected.

**TENACIOUS** adj. *persistent in holding on (as "barnacles are tenacious"); retentive (as "a tenacious mind")* n. **tenacity**, **courage**
If I had a more *tenacious* mind, I'd be able to remember history dates and math formulas better. Luckily, I'm a pretty *tenacious* wrestler—a real bulldog.

**BENEVOLENT** adj. *showing good will (Also from bene = good are benefactor, benign, beneficent, etc.)*
In world history we studied Charlemagne, an educated and *benevolent* French king who ruled for the good of his people. We debated the virtues of a *benevolent* dictatorship in class.

## MEMORY FIX
To learn these new words, write each one on a sheet of paper. Also write a synonym or definition for each and say the words aloud as you work.

## FIND THE SYNONYM
From the choices offered below, select the missing synonym for each word group and write it in the space provided.

| | | | | |
|---|---|---|---|---|
| astute | resilient | tenacious | alleviate | tenet |
| profound | formidable | meticulous | untenable | |

1. awesome   inspiring fear   redoubtable _____

2. deeply intellectual   all-encompassing _____

3. indefensible   unable to be inhabited _____

4. belief  dogma  principle  doctrine _____

5. able to spring back to form  elastic _____

6. perceptive  shrewd  wise  perspicacious _____

7. extremely careful  attentive to detail _____

8. persistent  determined  retentive _____

9. relieve  lessen  lighten  reduce _____

## TRUE OR FALSE
Read each sentence to see if it makes sense. Then mark **T** (true) or **F** (false) beside each.

1. Every bit of homework requires *indefatigable* effort. _____

2. By definition, a *benefactor* is usually *benevolent*. _____

3. Being *meticulous* about your appearance for a job interview is probably a waste of time. _____

4. If you insert the end of a stout board beneath that boulder, you'll have the *leverage* needed to move the rock. _____

5. The cult leader's insistence that he was Jesus Christ put him in an *untenable* position. _____

6. No one bothers to try to *alleviate* the symptoms of poison ivy.

   _____

7. Typically, *painstaking* folks are among the most prized in hospital operating rooms. _____

8. Rarely can you arrive at a *judicious* decision in seconds. _____

9. If you have to have a tumor, let's hope it's *benign*. _____

**10.** *Discerning* which chocolate chip cookies should win the blue ribbon would be a disgusting job. _____

**11.** The last quality you'd want in a fight is *tenacity*. _____

# ANALOGIES

Circle the one word pair in each list below that expresses the same relationship as the pair in capital letters.

**1. LAWYER : ASTUTE**
- (A) artist : insightful
- (B) chemist : beneficent
- (C) pathologist : painstaking
- (D) instructor : resilient
- (E) detective : awe-inspiring

**2. PROFOUND : THOUGHTFUL**
- (A) meticulous : painstaking
- (B) judicious : discreet
- (C) shrewd : astute
- (D) sagacious : bright
- (E) fearful : terrified

**3. SUPREME COURT : SAGACITY**
- (A) swimmer : tenacity
- (B) bones : tension
- (C) symphony : benevolence
- (D) muscles : resilience
- (E) city council : tenure

**4. FORMIDABLE : DEFENSE**
- (A) indefatigable : enemy
- (B) perspicacious : tenant
- (C) judicious : friend
- (D) discernible : traitor
- (E) redoubtable : warrior

**Answers for this chapter begin on page 200.**

# PAIRS OF POPULAR OPPOSITES

---

abstract/concrete • lax/stringent • atrophy/burgeon • affluent/indigent • cacophony/euphony • optimism/ pessimism • gravity/levity • desecrate/consecrate • resolute/irresolute • objective/subjective • refutable/ irrefutable

---

**ABSTRACT** adj. *indefinite; vague; theoretical; intangible*
**CONCRETE** adj. *definite or specific; real, tangible*
When I watch our team captain wrestle, I'm seeing a *concrete* display of courage, which is itself an *abstract* concept. Friendship is another *abstraction*, but my friends are real, *concrete* human beings.

**LAX** adj. *loose; unstructured; not firm; negligent; slack*
**STRINGENT** adj. *tight or constricted; rigid, adhering firmly to accepted standards*
At orientation for new counselors, the camp director handed us a *stringent* set of rules for the camp. "If rules are dangerously *lax*," he said, "we have a dangerous camp."

**ATROPHY** v. *to wither, degenerate; to waste away*
**BURGEON** v. *to flourish; to grow and quickly expand; bloom*
Ideas *burgeon* in people's minds just as flowers or weeds *burgeon* in soil. By contrast, anything that *atrophies* is faring poorly, like muscles that *atrophy* from illness.

**AFFLUENT** adj. *wealthy in a material sense*
**INDIGENT** adj. *very poor; lacking necessary material goods*
A guest lecturer at our school spoke on the contrast between Haiti's few *affluent* people and all the others—people so *indigent* that they live on the hills in three-sided shacks.

---

**PHON = sound**

phonics—*a system of sounds for letters, groups of letters, and syllables; acoustics, the science of sound*
> learned *phonics* early in school
> a new *phonics* system

symphony—*harmonious musical composition; symphony orchestra*
> beauty of a Beethoven *symphony*
> the Boston *Symphony*

Also: **telephone, sousaphone, phonetics, phonograph, euphony, cacophony**

---

**CACOPHONY** n. *displeasing, harsh sound; horrible noise*
**EUPHONY** n. *pleasing or sweet sound; harmony (of speech)*
Parents and kids have different ideas about *euphonious* sound. Our folks often call our music *cacophony* when it is absolute *euphony* to us. Any judgment about *cacophony* versus *euphony* seems pretty subjective.

**OPTIMISM** n. *a positive, upbeat, favorable outlook on life*
**PESSIMISM** n. *a negative, discouraging outlook on life*
For Mark Twain, Tom Sawyer represented *optimism*. Huck Finn, who was a stark realist, embodied *pessimism*. Comics joke that a *pessimist* is a person who has all the facts. An *optimist*, of course, focuses on the encouraging facts.

---

**SACR/SECR/SANC = sacred, holy**

sacrilege—*the desecration (profaning) of something holy*
> the inescapable *sacrilege* of war
> his swearing, a *sacrilege*

sanctity—*holiness, sacredness*
> the *sanctity* of the church
> for the *sanctity* of her soul

Also: **sacrosanct, inner sanctum, sacred, consecrate, desecrate**

---

**GRAVITY** n. *weighty importance; seriousness*
**LEVITY** n. *lightness of approach or treatment; humor*
We probably should treat the SATs with *gravity*, as the results can make a big difference in our lives. But I'm not just a number, and my score doesn't say who I am. My friends and I joke about SATs a lot, because *levity* helps us get past tough challenges.

**DESECRATE** v. *to defile or profane something sacred or very special*
**CONSECRATE** v. *to make sacred or holy or worthy of respect; to hallow*
Most Americans don't want anyone to *desecrate* our flag, our national anthem, or our monuments—anything that has special, emotional significance to us. Those things have been *consecrated* over time in our culture.

**RESOLUTE** adj. *firmly determined; steady; faithful*
**IRRESOLUTE** adj. *uncertain about behavior; vacillating*
I acted in a totally *resolute* manner last Halloween when I took some neighbor kids through a famous "haunted house." If I'd seemed nervous or *irresolute* for even a second, those kids would have bolted like spooked horses.

**OBJECTIVE** adj. *lacking personal feeling or involvement; in a detached, unbiased, fair manner*
**SUBJECTIVE** adj. *colored by personal feeling or opinion*
All kids wish that the grading of writing were more *objective* than it is; unfortunately, *subjective* factors always creep in. Our English teachers mark one grade on papers for the *objective* items like grammar, with a separate grade for creativity, which is a more *subjective* judgment.

**REFUTABLE** adj. *shaky in foundation, therefore able to be refuted (proved wrong or false)*
**IRREFUTABLE** adj. *impossible to refute (prove wrong or false)*
My lawyer cousin said he's only interested in *irrefutable* evidence that can't be disproved in court. *Refutabe* evidence is clearly worthless.

## MEMORY FIX

To learn these new words, write each one on a sheet of paper. Also write a synonym or definition for each and say the words aloud as you work.

## WORD ANALYSIS

Fill in the blanks in the sentences below based on this chapter's word list.

1. Euphonious sound makes you feel _____,
   contrasted with cacophony, which is _____.

2. The _____ sees the glass as half full; the
   _____ sees it as half empty.

3. Psychologists say that somewhat _____, depend-
   able rules provide children the necessary "fences" needed for
   security, whereas _____, unstable guidelines
   undermine their security.

4. _____ judgments are unclouded by emotion,
   whereas _____ judgments reflect the feelings of
   the judge.

5. A poem is a _____ thing; poetry itself, an
   _____ idea.

6. We speak of plants as things that _____ and
   grow, then eventually wither. Ideas or muscles that waste away or
   wither are said to _____ from lack of use.

7. The _____ '80s saw people busily acquiring
   luxuries, not just the necessities of life, which
   _____ people lack.

8. Humor provides the _____ that enables us to
   survive the _____ of situations beyond our
   control.

9. We _____ the senior medallion in the entryway
   of our school with a solemn ceremony. Any underclassman who
   _____ it will be dead meat.

10. Mom's _____ skill with homemade brownies was proved at the last bake sale. Now, if she says we don't need her brownies at a bake sale, that notion will be easily

    _____.

11. The Cowardly Lion was a timid, _____ fellow in the Oz books, but as soon as he had courage he behaved in a most _____ manner, full of determination.

## USING THE WORDS

Write the new words from this chapter on the correct lines below.

1. to wither away = _____
   to flourish, bloom = _____

2. can't be proved wrong = _____
   apt to be disproved = _____

3. impersonal = _____
   colored by feeling = _____

4. to profane = _____
   to hallow = _____

5. vague, indefinite = _____
   definite, real = _____

6. loose, lenient = _____
   tight, rigid = _____

7. horrible noise = _____
   pleasing sound = _____

8. rosy outlook – _____
   negative outlook = _____

9. seriousness = _____

   lightness, humor = _____

10. firmly determined = _____

    unsure, vacillating = _____

**Answers for this chapter begin on page 201.**

# THE BLUES

---

**irascible • writhe • taciturn • tawdry • servile • surreptitious • rancor • sullen • remorse • rue • malice • malign**

---

**IRASCIBLE** adj. *easily angered; testy, choleric, touchy*
*Irascible* after her bath at the vet's, Meatloaf snarled at Dude and me and then hid under the sofa. Poor Meatloaf. She's usually a pussycat, not an *irascible* grouch.

**WRITHE** v. *to twist; twist sideways in pain or suffering*
*Writhing* from side to side is the natural movement of snakes like the Southwestern sidewinder. When people *writhe*, they are either suffering pain or perhaps dancing. I've done a bit of *writhing* myself, on the wrestling mat.

**TACITURN** adj. *naturally silent, untalkative; laconic*
A *taciturn* person would enjoy this George Eliot quote: "Blessed be the person who has nothing to say who refrains from giving wordy evidence to that fact."

**TAWDRY** adj. *cheap-looking; showy, gaudy* n. **tawdry,** *showy, cheap finery*
*Tawdry* is a bit of British history that became a word. St. Audrey's laces were wispy silk necklaces sold for the saint's feast day. The words St. Audrey were run together, and *'taudrey's* laces were actually cheap and showy, so a new word gradually evolved.

**SERVILE** adj. *subservient, abject, annoyingly submissive*
Amy's latest role cast her as a *servile* maid who is always whining, "Anythin' more, yer lordship?" I dislike that *servile*, cringing attitude because it seems hypocritical.

**SURREPTITIOUS** adj. *secretive, deceptive; clandestine*
Does everybody take *surreptitious* little bites of cookie dough? Or *surreptitious* peeks at letters not addressed to them?

---

**MON/MONIT = warn, advise, remind**

**admonish**—*to warn strongly, reprove; show disapproval*
she *admonished* the kittens not to lose their mittens

**premonition**—*forewarning or foreboding; presentiment*
a *premonition* of disaster
troubled by *premonitions*

Also: **admonition, monitor, remonstrate, monument**

---

**RANCOR** n. *deep-seated bitterness; old enmity*
I've seen this cliché several times: "He viewed his old foe with *rancor*," and I know from experience that *rancor* is a bitter feeling.

**SULLEN** adj. *quietly resentful; lowering; gloomy, dismal*
For an understanding of the word *sullen*, it's hard to beat Robert Burns's lines in *Tam o'Shanter*: "Whare sits our sulky, *sullen* dame, Gathering her brows like gathering storm, Nursing her wrath to keep it warm."

**REMORSE** adj. *self-reproach, regret; a guilty uneasiness*
I feel some *remorse* if I squash a ladybug, because they're harmless, but I never regret flattening a wasp or bumblebee. I doubt that a wasp feels *remorse* when it stings me.

**RUE** v. *to regret exceedingly; feel remorse or sorrow*
Gramma is always saying I'll "*rue* the day" I became a car owner, and the poet A. E. Housman warned that giving your heart to a girl results in "endless *rue*." If I believe them, I'll be regretting something all my life!

---

**MEDI = middle**

**mediate**—*to reconcile by acting as an intermediary or go-between in a dispute*
happy to *mediate* for both sides
involved in *mediation*

**mediocre**—*of only ordinary quality or low quality*
unfortunately *mediocre* performance
only *mediocre* at best

Also: **mediator, intermediate, medium, medieval**

---

**MALICE** n. *the desire to see another suffer; extreme ill will or spite* adj. **malicious**
A disillusioned Mark Twain wrote in his *Autobiography*: "Of the entire brood, he [man] is the only one—the solitary one—that possesses *malice*. That is the basest of all instincts, passions, vices—the most hateful . . . He is the only creature that inflicts pain for sport, knowing it to *be* pain. . . .''

**MALIGN** n. *to slander, defame; speak of in an ill-willed manner*
Although we've published critical profiles in the school paper, we've never actually *maligned* anyone's character. Tabloids thrive on *maligning* famous people, but our staff regards that as yellow journalism.

## MEMORY FIX
To learn these new words, write each one on a sheet of paper. Also write a synonym or definition for each and say the words aloud as you work.

## FILL IN THE BLANKS
From the new words and roots in this chapter, select the one that best fits the meaning and logic of each phrase.

1. an _____, demanding boss who quickly lost her temper

2. still brooded on it years later, consumed by _____

3. an uneasy _____ that something would go wrong

4. reading the book _____ under the covers at night

5. reduced a touching story to a cheap, _____ thriller

6. gave us a cheerful, forgiving look, not a _____ one

7. _____ on the sidewalk in pain after spraining an ankle

8. working at replacing with charity the _____ he once felt

9. a naturally withdrawn, _____ personality who feels little need for talk

10. wearing the typical _____ look of a sycophant or toady

11. spoken with cruelty and _____, meant to be hurtful

12. to feel strong regret or remorse is to _____ something

## MATCHING

For each word in column A, find two synonymous words or phrases in column B and write their letters on the appropriate lines at the left.

| | A | B | |
|---|---|---|---|
| _____ | 1. remorse | a. slander | k. forewarning |
| _____ | | b. laconic | l. quietly resentful |
| _____ | 2. premonition | c. bitterness | m. guilty unease |
| _____ | | d. cheap | n. defame |
| _____ | 3. malign | e. secretive | o. deceptive |
| _____ | | f. foreboding | p. lowering |
| _____ | 4. sullen | g. subservient | q. silent |
| _____ | | h. self-reproach | r. choleric |
| _____ | 5. rancor | i. testy | s. gaudy |
| _____ | | j. abject | t. old enmity |
| _____ | 6. tawdry | | |
| _____ | | | |
| _____ | 7. surreptitious | | |
| _____ | | | |
| _____ | 8. taciturn | | |
| _____ | | | |
| _____ | 9. servile | | |
| _____ | | | |
| _____ | 10. irascible | | |
| _____ | | | |

## RHYME TIME

Complete these couplets of pretty awful poetry* with the correct form of one of the new words in this chapter.

1. It's me and Jane Fonda, lean and lithe,
   But some days this twist is a painful _____.

2. Regretful, sorrowful, sorry Sue,
   Hers is a heart laden with _____.

3. Children are _____ in Mother Goose rhyme,
   To be careful, watch out, and be home on time.

4. Nasty and mean was witchy old Alice,
   Her mind just brimmed with spite and _____.

5. Folks whose mental skills are _____
   Should perhaps think twice before playing poker.

6. To _____ is to resolve a dispute,
   By compromise, not by acting cute.

**Answers for this chapter begin on page 201.**

---

* Okay, *terrible* poetry.

# LISTS 6–10 REVIEW

Reviewing is the best way to keep these words forever. First, reread lists 6–10, saying each word aloud. You, too, may be someone who learns best through your ears.

## FIND THE SYNONYM

From the choices offered below, find the missing synonym for each word group and write it in the space provided.

| | | | |
|---|---|---|---|
| obsecure | immutable | mitigate | burgeon |
| lucid | respite | abstract | taciturn |
| astute | parsimonious | sacrilege | resolute |

1. dark  vague  mysterious  remote _____

2. alleviate  ease  relieve  lessen _____

3. unchanging  eternal  unalterable _____

4. break  rest  pause  lull _____

5. stingy  penny-pinching  miserly _____

6. distinct  clear  sensible  intelligible _____

7. perspicacious  shrewd  wise  perceptive _____

8. indefinite  theoretical  intangible _____

9. flourish  grow  blossom  bloom _____

10. determined  faithful  steady _____

11. desecration  fouling  profaning _____

12. laconic  silent  untalkative  reticent _____

## ANALOGIES

Circle the one word pair in each list below that expresses the same relationship as the pair in capital letters.

1. **SYMPHONY : VIOLINS**
   - (A)  admonition : manager
   - (B)  council : agenda
   - (C)  choir : music
   - (D)  religion : tenet
   - (E)  jury : oath

2. **ENERGY : TORPOR**
   - (A)  holiness : consecration
   - (B)  government : anarchy
   - (C)  phonics : speech
   - (D)  thought : discernment
   - (E)  heaviness : gravity

3. **SIN : REMORSEFUL**
   - (A)  shack : tawdry
   - (B)  mistake : rueful
   - (C)  carelessness : marred
   - (D)  problem : refuted
   - (E)  error : hopeful

4. **PAST : NOSTALGIA**
   - (A)  time : abstraction
   - (B)  sun : zenith
   - (C)  present : pessimism
   - (D)  philosophy : perusal
   - (E)  future : optimism

5. **MEDIATE : SAGE**
   - (A)  placate : sister
   - (B)  meander : guide
   - (C)  elucidate : teacher
   - (D)  posit : parent
   - (E)  refute : director

6. **BATTLE : TREPIDATION**
   - (A)  acquaintance : levity
   - (B)  general : hierarchy
   - (C)  enemy : rancor
   - (D)  dispute : gravity
   - (E)  sorrow : reticence

## MATCHING ANTONYMS
Knowing opposites is helpful. Match the words in column A with their antonyms in column B.

|  | A | B |
|---|---|---|
| _____ | 1. predecessor | lax |
| _____ | 2. affluent | malicious |
| _____ | 3. gravity | scan |
| _____ | 4. stringent | ignore |
| _____ | 5. resilience | heir |
| _____ | 6. benevolent | temerity |
| _____ | 7. placate | indigent |
| _____ | 8. peruse | silly |
| _____ | 9. heed | irritate |
| _____ | 10. judiciousness | levity |
| _____ | 11. profound | even-tempered |
| _____ | 12. irascible | rigidity |

## FILL IN THE BLANKS
From the choices offered below, select the word that best completes the meaning and logic of each sentence. Be sure to put each word into the correct grammatical form.

| volition | tenacious | raze | obliterate | |
|---|---|---|---|---|
| garner | reticent | virtuoso | quandary | |
| rebuff | irrefutable | meticulous | proponent | zenith |

1. A glance at Amy's trophies and you'd think her whole goal in life was to _____ swimming awards.

2. Even after several months, I'm still as _____ about the upkeep of my old used car as I was at first.

3. My friend Juan is _____ on every topic but music, the one subject that really loosens his tongue.

4.  I wish that females understood how afraid guys are of being
    _____ when they call girls for dates.

5.  A wrecking crew _____ the old theater and
    carted away all the debris, thus _____ all traces
    of the structure.

6.  In Dicken's *A Tale of Two Cities*, Sydney Carton goes to the
    gallows of his own _____ in order to save
    another man's life and thereby secure a woman's happiness.

7.  Our neighbors were in a _____ over what to call
    their new French restaurant until Dad suggested "Le Snail."

8.  "Well, Meatloaf," Mom said accusingly, "these feathered corpses
    are _____ evidence of what you did last night!"

9.  Martin Luther King was one of the most eloquent
    _____ of equality of opportunity for all Americans.

10. To study tennis _____, look at some old clips of
    Arthur Ashe, Martina Navratilova, and John McEnroe.

11. As one who remembers everything she's read, my Aunt Jolly must
    have one of the world's most _____ minds.

12. Michael Jackson reached the _____ of his career
    at a very young age compared with most performers.

**Answers for this review lesson begin on page 202.**

# VACILLATE NOT!

---

acclaim • rejuvenate • revere • sanction • temper • saturate • whet • scrutinize • vacillate • thwart • venerate • waive

---

**ACCLAIM** v. *to proclaim or announce with noisy approval, such as shouts and applause* n. **acclaim** and **acclamation**
The first time he was in a dog show, Dude found the *acclaim* he loves. When he was *acclaimed* as Best of Breed in the Yorkshire terrier class, he strutted in front of the audience with obvious delight in their applause.

**REJUVENATE** v. *to make youthful or like new again; to renew or reinvigorate*
The restoration of my old secondhand car has *rejuvenated* it entirely. "You've accomplished a total *rejuvenation*," Dad told me, gazing at it with admiration.

**REVERE** v. *to respect and honor; to venerate, worship* n. **reverence**
For the Puritans, the words *revere, respect,* and *venerate* described much of their lives. They taught their children to *revere* God, their country, adults, and one another.

**SANCTION** v. *to confirm, authorize; endorse, approve, support* n. **sanction**, *authorization, approval* n. **sanctions**, *forceful measures to assure compliance with law (usu. international)*
Although Senior Skip Day is an old tradition, our principal has said, "I can't *sanction* it, although I'll probably condone it again. Obviously, no principal can *sanction* the breaking of school rules."

**TEMPER** v. *to moderate or adjust as conditions require; or, to strengthen through hardship*
In his inaugural address, John F. Kennedy referred to Americans as a people "*tempered* by war, disciplined by a hard and bitter peace." Thirty years later, we are trying to *temper* our military needs and attend to other urgent problems.

---

**CLAM/CLAIM = to shout, cry out**

clamor—*great outcry or shouting; noisy or confused demand*
   the *clamor* of his fans
   all *clamoring* for attention

disclaim—*to deny or disavow; speak in denial; repudiate*
   *disclaim* all knowledge
   file a *disclaimer* (legal denial)

Also: **acclaim, exclamation, exclaim, proclaim, proclamation, declaim, declamation, reclaim, reclamation**

---

**SATURATE** v. *to fill completely; satiate, soak*
If I study in Spain for a college semester, I can *saturate* myself with Spanish. The best way to learn any language is by total immersion or *saturation*.

**WHET** v. *to excite or stimulate (the mind or appetite); to hone or sharpen (a knife or mind)*
In *Sea Fever*, poet John Masefield wrote, "I must down to the seas again, to the vagrant gypsy life, To the gull's way and the whale's way, where the wind's like a *whetted* knife." Great old poems like that *whet* everyone's appetite for more.

**SCRUTINIZE** v. *to examine minutely, with close attention* n. scrutiny, *close examination*
Now that Dude's in dog shows occasionally, we've learned to *scrutinize* him from head to tail before judging. He seems to enjoy being *scrutinized*, probably because he's so vain.

---

**PLEX/PLIC/PLY = to fold**

imply—*to suggest or hint without stating directly*
   *implied* I ought to diet
   stung by her *implication*

explicit—*fully and precisely revealed; without question*
   follow her *explicit* orders
   a need for you to be *explicit*

Also: **complex, complicate, comply, implication, explicate, reply, replicate, replica**

---

**VACILLATE** v. *to fluctuate; to change from one opinion to another; also, to hesitate*
"People who *vacillate* drive me right up the wall," Dad says. "I work better with definite, confident people, not folks who are *vacillating* like a bunch of dithering birds!"

**THWART** v. *to foil, baffle, or frustrate (someone's attempts)*
A young Yorky named Princess has pranced onto the show dog scene and may *thwart* Dude's chances for Best of Breed next year. Having been *thwarted* myself in wrestling matches, I know how tough it is to come in second-best.

**VENERATE** v. *to revere, respect, and admire with deference* adj. **venerable**, *worthy of respect*
No matter how he acted, King Henry VIII of Britain expected his subjects to *venerate* him. Today's royal family, to the open dismay of the *venerable* Elizabeth II, is forfeiting its right to *veneration* by behavior no longer overlooked.

**WAIVE** v. *to give up voluntarily; relinquish; forgo or postpone*
An obviously guilty student *waived* his right to a trial in student court. My family has a home court, but no one ever yields without being heard; we're all too independent to *waive* a chance at justifying our actions.

## MEMORY FIX
To learn these new words, write each one on a sheet of paper. Also write a synonym or definition for each and say the words aloud as you work.

## SUBSTITUTION
Replace each italicized word or phrase with the correct word from the list of words in this chapter, including words from roots.

1. "Fresh paint and wallpaper will absolutely *make like new again* this old apartment," Mom told our elderly aunt.

   _____

2. "Quit *shilly-shallying* and dive in," the swim coach yelled.

   _____

3. "Are you *hinting* that I dye my hair?" Aunt Jolly teased as she patted her bright red-orange curls. _____

4. Consideration for others' feelings sometimes causes us to *adjust as conditions demand* honesty with thoughtfulness.

   _____

5. After her astonishing victory in the relay, Amy was greeted with *noisy shouts of approval.* _____

6. Confucius taught his followers to *respect and honor* their elders.

   _____

7. Mom and Amy *carefully examined* the menu before ordering giant taco salads. _____

8. "I absolutely *refuse to acknowledge* any dog this muddy," Mom said, grinning at filthy little Dude. _____

9. A recent class debate focused on the *legal restrictions* against whaling in U.S. waters, because we can no longer *endorse or authorize* killing those endangered mammals.

   _____

10. A brief explanation of the case showed us why the defendant had *relinquished* his right to a trial by jury. _____

## FIND THE ODDBALL

In each word group, cross out the oddball, the one unrelated word or phrase.

1. fill up   satiate   sponge   soak   saturate

2. twist   sharpen   excite   stimulate   whet

3. thwart   flinch   frustrate   foil   baffle

4. dankness   clamor   outcry   shouting   uproar

5. implied   fully revealed   precise   explicit   unquestionable

6. defer to   venerate   honor   deter   revere

7. urge   support   authorize   endorse   sanction

8. repudiate   deny   discourage   disavow   disclaim

9. forgo   yield willingly   relinquish   relegate   waive

10. reject   inspect   scrutinize   examine   study carefully

## TRUE OR FALSE

Read each sentence to see how the words in this chapter are being used. Then mark **T** (true) or **F** (false) beside each sentence.

1. Medication doesn't need to come with *explicit* advice. _____

2. You should *thwart* the baby's attempt to ride a tricycle down the porch steps. _____

3. It's great when your idea meets with universal *acclaim.* _____

4. Just as steel is *tempered* for strength, so are survival skills *tempered* during hard times. _____

5. Exciting previews *whet* our desire to see a movie. _____

6. Sleeping people appreciate a soothing *clamor* nearby. _____

7. Avoid being *saturated* with knowledge before exams. _____

8. You can't *rejuvenate* road pizza. _____

**Answers for this chapter begin on page 202.**

# HOW MUCH IS A DEARTH?

---

**brevity • criterion • delineate • ephemeral • copious • dearth • evanescent • paucity • prodigious • meager • redundant • scanty**

---

**BREVITY** n. *shortness, briefness; conciseness of expression*
In *Hamlet* our class found this famous quotation: "*Brevity* is the soul of wit." And in Coleridge's poetry we found: "What is an Epigram? a dwarfish whole, Its body *brevity* and wit its soul." Coleridge and Shakespeare probably would have laughed at the same short jokes.

**CRITERION** n. *a standard used for making judgments* pl. **criteria**
After all the basic *criteria* for judging dogs have been satisfied, a judge looks for a happy, friendly dog. For pet owners, temperament is always the most important *criterion* for evaluating a dog.

**DELINEATE** v. *to portray accurately; outline, describe*
The guidance counselor *delineated* the various aspects of college applications. She concentrated most on the essays, with a careful *delineation* of the criteria for a good essay.

**EPHEMERAL** adj. *short-lived, fleeting, transient*
It's good that mosquitoes, gnats, and flies have *ephemeral* lives. But my time in high school is beginning to seem pretty *ephemeral* too, and that's not so good.

**COPIOUS** adj. *superabundant; in plentiful supply*
Our yard has a *copious* supply of moles, which are awfully destructive. We're waiting for Meatloaf-the-Assassin to turn that *copious* number into a dearth.

---

**MIN = less, little**

**minuscule**—*very, very small*
a *minuscule* insect
a pitiful, *minuscule* effort

**mince**—*to chop very fine; to walk or talk in an affected way*
*mince* the onions
she *minced* her way down the aisle

Also: **minus, diminish, diminution, minority, miniature**

---

# DEARTH n. *scarcity or lack; paucity*
Our class debated the poet Keats's comment on "the inhuman *dearth* of noble natures" and disagreed with Keats. "There's no *dearth* of good people," our teacher said, "but it's the other kind who make headlines."

# EVANESCENT adj. *fading or vanishing quickly, like vapor; transient* n. evanescence
Ghosts are naturally *evanescent*, or so the story goes. I was a Halloween trick-or-treat ghost years ago, but a guy under a sheet isn't nearly as *evanescent* as he'd like to be.

# PAUCITY n. *lack or scarcity of number or amount*
The word *paucity* is rarely used, except on SATs or PSATs. I often read about the "lack of" something or that "only a few exist," but for standardized tests, *paucity* lives on. Sigh.

---

**MAGN = great, large**

**magnanimous**—*generously forgiving; big-spirited*
a *magnanimous* gesture
the *magnanimous* nature of his soul

**magnate**—*someone of power, rank, or influence*
an oil *magnate*
the current banking *magnate*

Also: **magnify, magnificent, magnitude, magnanimity**

---

**PRODIGIOUS** adj. *inspiring awe; enormous in size or capacity*
Dinosaurs were creatures of *prodigious* size and exotic appearance, two qualities that fascinate. Children especially have a *prodigious* appetite for facts about dinosaurs.

**MEAGER** adj. *lacking in quality or quantity; scanty, skimpy, spare, sparse* also, **meagre**
I have used *meager* to describe tons of things. For instance: a narrow house on a *meager* lot; an old woman, *meager* of frame and stooped; he made only a *meager* effort; and why did you give me such a *meager* amount of spaghetti when I'm starving?

**REDUNDANT** adj. *extra and unnecessary; superfluous; unneeded* n. **redundancy**
*Redundancies* are tautological expressions that drive editors nuts. For example, "young kitten" and "young foal" are *redundant* because kitten and foal refer only to animals that are young. Also, "first and foremost" is a *redundant* expression.

**SCANTY** adj. *brief or short; lacking desired amount or size; meager*
I thought I liked *scanty* swimsuits until I saw my girlfriend in the *scantiest* bikini on earth. I instantly became Mister Jealous Boyfriend and said she couldn't wear that *scanty* excuse for a suit where anyone else could see her.

## MEMORY FIX
To learn these new words, write each one on a sheet of paper. Also write a synonym or definition for each and say the words aloud as you work.

## FILL IN THE BLANKS
From the new words in this chapter, select the one that best completes the meaning and logic of each sentence. Use the correct form of the word.

1. In order to choose a winner fairly, all contestants must be judged on the same _____.

2. Please _____ which topics to cover in this essay.

3. Will there ever be a day when there's a _____ of problems and a _____ supply of good answers?

4. Amy _____ across the stage, self-conscious from head to toe.

5. An affluent newspaper _____ funds ten scholarships.

## MATCHING

Circle the two words or phrases that best explain the meaning of each word in bold type.

1. **brevity**
   (A) description
   (B) briefness
   (C) humor
   (D) conciseness

2. **delineate**
   (A) draw freehand
   (B) show artistically
   (C) outline
   (D) portray accurately

3. **prodigious**
   (A) wasteful
   (B) immense
   (C) enormous
   (D) liberal

4. **dearth**
   (A) scarcity
   (B) ground
   (C) paucity
   (D) soil

5. **ephemeral**
   (A) fleeting
   (B) transient
   (C) beautiful
   (D) sorrowful

6. **meager**
   (A) narrow-minded
   (B) Tarzan growl
   (C) scanty
   (D) skimpy

7. **redundant**
   (A) clamorous
   (B) unnecessary
   (C) dimwitted
   (D) superfluous

8. **magnanimous**
   (A) generous in spirit
   (B) large rodent
   (C) uncomfortably large
   (D) big-hearted

## WORDS IN CONTEXT

Write the meaning of each italicized word on the lines provided.

**1.** certainly the most important *criterion* for acceptance

_____

**2.** wealthy oil *magnate* from the Middle East

_____

**3.** the *evanescent* fragrance of perfume

_____

**4.** a list of *copious* complaints

_____

**5.** only a *minuscule* amount of whipped cream

_____

**6.** shouldn't *mince* words with her

_____

**7.** enjoyed the depth and *brevity* of his talk

_____

**8.** King Arthur's legendary *magnanimous* nature

_____

**9.** numerous *redundant* sentences to be cut

_____

**10.** renovation demanded a *prodigious* amount of energy

_____

# MATCHING ANTONYMS

In the column on the right, find two antonyms for each word at the left.

| | | |
|---|---|---|
| _____ | 1. ephemeral | copious |
| _____ | | scanty |
| _____ | 2. copious | meager |
| _____ | | tiny |
| _____ | 3. scanty | abundant |
| _____ | | superabundance |
| _____ | 4. dearth | plentiful amount |
| _____ | | enduring |
| _____ | 5. prodigious | minuscule |
| _____ | | long-lived |

**Answers for this chapter begin on page 203.**

# LIST 13

# AN ECLECTIC COLLECTION

---

aesthetic • eclectic • gratuitous • inevitable • irony •
expedient • apocryphal • heinous • mundane •
arduous • prodigal • quixotic

---

**AESTHETIC** adj. *referring to a sense of beauty; artistic*
Poet James Terry White recognized the importance of *aesthetic* needs, recommending that you "buy hyacinths to feed thy soul." Flowers are *aesthetically* necessary to some; others, like me, need music or time alone in a wilderness area.

**ECLECTIC** adj. *carefully selected from many good sources*
I have a small but *eclectic* assortment of tapes and CDs ranging from the Dead to Tchaikovsky. Amy says our house is furnished in an *eclectic* manner, but our stuff is really just a collection of hand-me-downs from a large family.

**GRATUITOUS** adj. *offered freely, but not necessary under the circumstances, therefore unwanted or unneeded*
I guess everyone with a big family has one relative known for *gratuitous* advice. Ours is Uncle Mort, who drops his *gratuitous* comments into every conversation.

**INEVITABLE** adj. *unavoidable*
Uncle Mort's steady string of helpful advice used to annoy me, but now I know it's *inevitable*. His verbal wind is just as *inevitable* as the wind outside.

**IRONY** n. *the opposite of what would be normal or expected; humor based on incongruity* adj. **ironic**
Mom says that the real *irony* about Uncle Mort is that he's so often right. Most *ironic* of all is his habit of being right about kids, although he has none himself.

---

**LEG/LECT/LIG = to choose, pick, read**

**predilection**—*natural preference; positive feelings for*
     cat's *predilection* for mice
     her *predilection* for jazz

**negligible**—*of only minor importance, if any*
     a *negligible* difference
     his influence was *negligible*

Also: **legion, legation, legible, illegible, legumes (beans and peas that are picked), eligible, select, legacy**

---

**EXPEDIENT** adj. *suitable, practical, or advisable; also, opportunistic* n. **expediency**
In history class we discussed the view that the bomb dropped on Hiroshima was an *expedient* action undertaken to end World War II. Many felt that *expediency* had obscured morality in that case, so we had a heated argument.

**APOCRYPHAL** adj. *of doubtful authorship; fictitious*
Highly visible or controversial people often have comments attributed to them that are *apocryphal*. Even so, *apocryphal* quotations have a habit of surviving.

**HEINOUS** adj. *shockingly awful, appalling; abominable, outrageous*
Cult leaders Jim Jones and David Koresh led their followers into death, thereby committing a *heinous* crime: murder. Mass murder of trusting people is as *heinous* as anything I can imagine.

---

**LEG = law**

**legitimate**—*correct by law; conforming to accepted procedure*
     a *legitimate* driver
     a logical, *legitimate* reason

**legislate**—*to formally enact as law; to rule legally*
     a recently *legislated* statute
     our state *legislature*

Also: **legal, illegal, legitimize, legate** *(official emissary)*

---

**MUNDANE** adj. *everyday, commonplace, like menial chores*
As the opposite of celestial or heavenly, anything *mundane* should be dull, but it isn't always. Washing the car is a *mundane* chore, but I like slopping around on a wet driveway.

**ARDUOUS** adj. *demanding, hard to achieve; strenuous*
Packing gear into a wilderness camping area seems *arduous* to some, but not to me and my friends. For my friend Rob, writing an essay is an *arduous* job.

**PRODIGAL** adj. *wildly extravagant or lavish in spending*
Mom and Dad don't talk about our government's *prodigal* spending; they yell. They feel strongly about using funds wisely, so none of us is *prodigal* with money.

**QUIXOTIC** adj. *extravagantly idealistic; unpredictable; unrealistic or imaginary*
The word *quixotic* comes from the character Don Quixote in Cervantes's novel, a story of a lovable, wacky old fellow who imagines that he's a knight. *Quixotic* ideas are strange, a little crazy, but often wonderful.

## MEMORY FIX
To learn these new words, write each one on a sheet of paper. Also write a synonym or definition for each and say the words aloud as you work.

## MATCHING
Match the words in column A with their meanings in column B and write the meanings in the spaces provided.

|  | A | B |
|---|---|---|
| _____ | 1. gratuitous | opportunistic |
| _____ | 2. inevitable | insanely idealistic |
| _____ | 3. expedient | abominable, appalling |
| _____ | 4. arduous | commonplace |
| _____ | 5. quixotic | unwanted or unneeded |
| _____ | 6. apocryphal | strenuous |
| _____ | 7. mundane | unavoidable |
| _____ | 8. heinous | of doubtful authorship |

## FILL IN THE BLANKS

From the words below, select the one that best completes the meaning and logic of this essay.

aesthetic   ironic   predilection   negligible
eclectic   prodigal   legislate   legitimate

Meatloaf's undisguised _____ for small, furry critters results in many "gifts" left on the porch for our family. Last year's presents from Meatloaf were a(n) _____ array of mice, moles, birds, and shrews. In the summer, Meatloaf was absolutely _____ with these offerings, which we found pretty gross as time went on.

There's no _____ reason for her to hunt." Mom fumed. "We feed her enough that she could ignore her cat instincts!" Both Mom and Amy wish we could _____ a cat's behavior, but cats adhere strictly to their own laws.

"No point in scolding. Anything you say to a cat has only a _____ effect on its behavior," Dad observed. "How _____ that we should love a hunter," he went on, "when we're such fervent pacifists."

Of course, the grace and beauty of cats appeal to the _____ senses of many people, not just to our family.

# ANALOGIES

Circle the one word pair in each list below that expresses the same relationship as the pair in capital letters.

1. **DAYDREAMING : QUIXOTIC**
   (A) bicycling : expedient
   (B) giving : prodigal
   (C) reading : legitimate
   (D) cleaning house : mundane
   (E) eating : aesthetic

2. **BAD : HEINOUS**
   (A) gratuitous : free
   (B) aesthetic : artistic
   (C) prodigal : scanty
   (D) proposed : legitimate
   (E) difficult : arduous

3. **APOCRYPHAL : LEGEND**
   (A) long-range : goal
   (B) fictitious : fable
   (C) inevitable : story
   (D) gratuitous : gossip
   (E) hero : prodigal

# FIND THE ANTONYM

Pair the words below with their antonyms by writing them on the correct lines.

| parsimonious | haphazard | significant | apocryphal |
| aversion | quixotic | customary | mundane |
| noble | desired | avoidable | impractical |

_____ 1. authentic

_____ 3. inevitable

_____ 4. gratuitous

_____ 5. negligible

_____ 6. predeliction

_____ 7. eclectic

_____ 8. heinous

_____ 9. ironic

_____ 10. heavenly

_____ 11. prodigal

_____ 12. expedient

**Answers for this chapter begin on page 203.**

# LIST 14 YAKKETY YAK

---

verbose • blasphemy • vilify • diatribe • vitriolic • jargon • satire • tirade • slander • garble • rhetoric • garrulous

---

**VERBOSE** adj. *using more words than necessary; wordy*
When the teacher writes *VERBOSE!* across the top of my paper, I know I got carried away with descriptions again. The sin of *verbosity* is shared by many writers, of course, Stephen King included.

**BLASPHEMY** n. *disrespect or irreverence toward something sacred or seriously important* n. **blaspheme**
Playwright George Bernard Shaw wrote in *Pygmalion*, "Independence? That's middle-class *blasphemy*. We are all dependent on one another, every soul of us on earth." And later he said, "All great truths begin as *blasphemies*."

**VILIFY** v. *to slander or defame someone's name or standing in the community; to malign* n. **vilification**
The tabloid papers you see in the grocery store will apparently *vilify* anyone in public life. Their *vilifications* of prominent figures make me shake my head and wonder.

**DIATRIBE** n. *bitter, critical speech or writing*
*Diatribes* flourish in politics, where people seem eager to criticize others. Negative, name-calling speeches were banned in our school elections so that anything resembling a *diatribe* was cut short.

**VITRIOLIC** adj. *burning or corrosive like acid; caustic*
Political activists sometimes give *vitriolic* speeches when they're trying to make a point. But hearing these emotional, *vitriolic* attacks usually turns me against the speaker.

---

**QUER/QUIR/QUIS = to ask, seek**

querulous—*complaining, fault-finding, fretful; petulant*
a *querulous* tone of voice
her repeated, *querulous* comments

inquisitive—*inquiring, questioning, curious*
an *inquisitive* mind
an *inquisitive* sort of person

Also: **acquire, acquisition, query, inquire, require, inquisition, perquisite (perk), exquisite, requisition, requisite**

---

**JARGON** n. *special language or terminology; dialect or hybrid language*
Every industry or specialty develops its own *jargon*—words and expressions that only the insiders know. Kids often develop a *jargon* that sets them apart from their parents.

**SATIRE** n. *comedy using laughter as a weapon to evoke a feeling of scorn along with amusement*
My history class is reading *Huckleberry Finn*, Twain's *satire* that ridicules the prejudice, stupidity, and hypocrisy in America in the mid-nineteenth century. Twain's insightful *satiric* pen gives us laughter along with truth.

**TIRADE** n. *a lengthy, emotional, critical speech*
Coaches tend to lapse into a *tirade* when a team player makes a serious mistake. For those who have to listen to them, *tirades* are extremely memorable.

---

**DIC/DICT = to speak, say; words**

indict—*to charge with an offense, in court or informally*
*indicted* for the crime of murder
*indicted* by my own family

edict—*a formal order or command; a command by law*
Mom's *edict* on bedtime
the governor's latest *edict*

Also: **dictate, predict, indicate, indicative, dictatorial, dictionary, dictaphone, dictator, predicate**

---

**SLANDER** n. *a false, defamatory spoken criticism of someone* v. *to defame with untrue speech*
While libel can be either written or oral, *slander* refers to nasty, personal criticism that is oral only. Both *slander* and libel can be grounds for a lawsuit.

**GARBLE** n. *to change or alter meaning through misrepresentation of facts or distortion of ideas*
If you want to *garble* a message, just play telephone as you did at kids' birthday parties. One *garbled* message I remember began as "Who's Superman?" and ended up "Where's Pooh's can?"

**RHETORIC** n. *insincere or high-flown writing or speech; originally, the study of good communication*
*Rhetoric* has degenerated from something admirable and worthy of study to something contemptible, as when we accuse someone of "mere *rhetoric*." A *rhetorical* question is one asked for effect, with little hope of a serious answer.

**GARRULOUS** adj. *extremely talkative, gabby, loquacious, verbose* n. **garrulity**
Our Aunt Jolly is pretty *garrulous*, but we enjoy her verbosity because it's funny and never cruel. *Garrulity* turns people off if it drones on in a negative, critical way.

## MEMORY FIX
Again, to learn these new words, write each one on a sheet of paper. Also write a synonym or definition for each and say the words aloud as you work.

## SUBSTITUTION
Replace each italicized word or phrase with the correct word from the list of words in this chapter, including words from roots.

1.  The teacher explained the assignment by asking several *just-for-effect* questions to get us thinking. _____

2.  Don't *badly interpret* that information, please.
    _____

3. His talk wasn't a lecture, it was a *bitter, critical speech* on the evils of drinking. _____

4. Jonathan Swift's most biting *comedy arousing scorn* was "A Modest Proposal," in which he suggested a grisly solution to the Irish famine. _____

5. "Have some dessert?" shrieked Amy. "When you know I'm dieting? That's an *unthinkable insult or disrespect!*"

   _____

6. Gabbing throughout dinner and the movie is one sure way to get yourself described as *extremely talkative.* _____

7. It's taking Mom and Dad a while to learn the *special language* that goes with computers. _____

8. After hearing the evidence, the jury *formally charged* the suspect on a charge of grand larceny. _____

9. As we watched the movie, I felt my youngest cousin grow tense during the evil Queen's *lengthy, emotional speech* against innocent Snow White. _____

10. Respectable newspapers are careful not to print *material that would damage someone's reputation.* _____

## TRUE OR FALSE

Read each sentence to see if it is correct. Then mark **T** (true) or **F** (false) beside each.

1. If you want folks to think you're a rocket scientist, you'll need a bit of rocketry *jargon.* _____

2. If people in the audience say, "Hmm, more *rhetoric,*" at the end of your speech, you'll feel proud. _____

3. When you're asking Dad if you can borrow the car, a *vitriolic* tone will probably work the best. _____

4. Swearing is unacceptable *blasphemy* to many people. _____

5. The cartoon strip *Doonesbury* uses *satire* to good advantage. _____

6. A *querulous* "Why aren't you up?" starts the day right. _____

7. Truly vicious *slander* can *vilify* a person almost beyond redemption. _____

## MATCHING
From the column on the right, select two synonyms or phrases that explain each of the words at the left and write in your answers.

| | | |
|---|---|---|
| _____ | 1. verbose | corrosive |
| _____ | | petulant |
| _____ | 2. vilify | wordy |
| _____ | | questioning |
| _____ | 3. querulous | defame |
| _____ | | legal order |
| _____ | 4. vitriolic | command |
| _____ | | malign |
| _____ | 5. edict | slander |
| _____ | | caustic |
| _____ | 6. inquisitive | curious |
| _____ | | garrulous |
| _____ | 7. slander | dishonor |
| _____ | | fretful |

**Answers for this chapter begin on page 204.**

# LIST 15

# WISHY-WASHY

ambiguous • capitulate • defer • ambivalence •
dubious • languor • fluctuate • tentative • indifferent •
lethargy • innocuous • stagnant

**AMBIGUOUS** adj. *indefinite, open to more than one interpretation; obscure, uncertain* n. **ambiguity**
When Mom asked if the snake was loose in the house, I gave an *ambiguous* reply to keep her from worrying. But Mom hates *ambiguity*, and she said, "Yes or no? Be definite!"

**CAPITULATE** v. *to give in, surrender, acquiesce*
I *capitulated* under pressure and admitted that the snake was somewhere in the house. I begged Mom to stay in her room until we'd found him, and she *capitulated* readily.

**DEFER** v. *to yield to someone of greater authority or age; to put off until another time* n. **deference**
After finding the snake wrapped around the warm coils of the refrigerator, we *deferred* to Mom's wishes and moved him to the garage. I can no longer *defer* making him a stout cage.

**AMBIVALENCE** n. *fluctuation between one thing and another; uncertainty or indecision*
People are rarely *ambivalent* about snakes; either they like them or not. Mom hasn't any *ambivalence* about them whatever and thinks they all belong in zoos.

**DUBIOUS** adj. *doubtful; of questionable truth or quality; suspicious*
Unfortunately, Mom regards my fondness for wildlife as a *dubious* character trait. When I adopted a box turtle, she said he was of *dubious* value as a pet.

---

**VAD/VAS = to go**

**evade**—*to avoid, dodge, or circumvent a person or issue*
    *evaded* the issue
    *evaded* detection
    her *evasive* answer

**pervade**—*to go throughout, to diffuse throughout, to permeate*
    hint of fear *pervaded* the room
    a *pervasive* odor of skunk

Also: **evasion, invade, invasion, pervasion**

---

**LANGUOR** n. *sluggishness; tiredness or weakness; lethargy* adj. **languid**
Cats are *languorous* animals, stretching and yawning sleepily in the sun, then flopping down to doze again. This *languor* is true of cats of all types; cats sleep more hours a day than most other animals.

**FLUCTUATE** v. *to shift up and down; or, to come and go, as ocean waves*
Newscasters report daily *fluctuations* in the stock market, in temperatures, and in public opinion on current topics. Emotions *fluctuate* too, of course, according to what's happening in our lives.

**TENTATIVE** adj. *hesitant, unsure, uncertain*
E. B. White, author of *Charlotte's Web* and coauthor of *The Elements of Style*, warns us about *tentative* writing. "Vigorous writing is concise," he says, "and definite." Prose hedged with qualifiers is not only *tentative*, of course, it's also more wordy.

---

**DUC/DUCT = to lead, direct**

**deduce**—*to conclude or infer by reasoned thought*
    *deduce* that from the evidence
    a clever *deduction*

**conducive**—*apt to promote or assist*
    atmosphere *conducive* to learning
    a bed *conducive* to rest

Also: **induce, induction, reduce, reduction, seduce, seduction, conduct, conduction, abduct, deduct**

---

**INDIFFERENT** adj. *not good or bad; unconcerned or not curious; aloof or detached; unbiased*
An *indifferent* student doesn't care about learning. Someone who regards flowers with an *indifferent* eye isn't interested in flowers. *Indifference* can extend all the way to total detachment.

**LETHARGY** n. *serious tiredness; languor, laziness, torpor*
The *lethargy* of cats is rooted in their physiological need for sleep because of hearts and lungs proportionately smaller than those of other animals. When on a chase, though, the *lethargic* cheetah is the fastest critter on land.

**INNOCUOUS** adj. *harmless; or, dull, insipid*
The school's play director said he was tired of doing safe, *innocuous* plays. This year's play may cause a few raised eyebrows, but it certainly isn't *innocuous*.

**STAGNANT** adj. *unmoving or not flowing (stagnant water); stale (stagnant air); inactive* v. **stagnate**
We've all seen *stagnant* ponds and met people who have let their minds *stagnate*. A new word was born about twenty years ago when *stagnation* married *inflation* and created *stagflation*, an economic term describing stubborn inflation blended with *stagnant* consumer demand and noticeable unemployment.

## MEMORY FIX
And again . . . hang in there and write each new word and a synonym or definition for each. Say the words aloud as you write them.

## WORDS IN CONTEXT
Write the meaning of each italicized word based on how it is used in its quotation.

1. George Bernard Shaw: "The worst sin towards our fellow creatures is not to hate them, but to be *indifferent* to them: that's the essence of inhumanity." _____

2. Samuel Johnson: "I will be conquered; I will not *capitulate*." 
_____

3. Francis Bacon: "*Defer* not charities till death." _____

4. President Grover Cleveland: "After an existence of nearly 20 years of almost *innocuous* desuetude [disuse] these laws are brought forth." _____

5. Percy Bysshe Shelley, "To A Skylark":
"With thy clear keen joyance
*Languor* cannot be." _____

6. William Wordsworth, "National Independence and Liberty":
"Milton! thou shouldst be living at this hour:
England hath need of thee; she is a fen
Of *stagnant* waters." _____

7. Sir Isaac Newton, ". . . whatever is not *deduced* from the phenomena is to be called an hypothesis." _____

## MATCHING
Circle the two words or phrases that best explain the meaning of each word in bold type.

1. **fluctuate**
   (A) vary up or down
   (B) group together in a flock
   (C) disturb
   (D) come and go

2. **dubious**
   (A) old musical refrain
   (B) suspicious
   (C) of doubtful quality
   (D) sneaky

3. **ambivalence**
   (A) versatility
   (B) medical vehicle
   (C) wishy-washiness
   (D) indecision

4. **tentative**
   (A) hesitant
   (B) unsure
   (C) camping term
   (D) timely

5. **lethargic**
   (A) revolting
   (B) languorous
   (C) sick
   (D) torpid

6. **ambiguous**
   (A) two-faced
   (B) enlarged
   (C) indefinite
   (D) uncertain

7. **evade**
   (A) avoid
   (B) hide
   (C) circumvent
   (D) fool

9. **pervade**
   (A) become weird
   (B) dole out
   (C) permeate
   (D) diffuse thr oughout

8. **conducive**
   (A) rewarding
   (B) promoting
   (C) punishing
   (D) assisting

## FIND THE SYNONYM

From the choices offered below, select the missing synonym for each word group and write it in the space provided.

capitulate   stagnant   defer   innocuous
languor      tentative   evade   indifferent

1. dodge   avoid   circumvent   be elusive _____

2. yield in respect   postpone   suspend   put off

   _____

3. sluggishness   weariness   torpor   lethargy _____

4. dull   harmless   insipid   inoffensive _____

5. stale   motionless   inactive   not flowing _____

6. unconcerned   detached   not curious   aloof

   _____

7. hesitant   undeveloped   unsure   uncertain

   _____

8. give in   yield   acquiesce   surrender _____

**Answers for this chapter begin on page 204.**

# LISTS 11–15 REVIEW

Quick, quick, a handy review before those new words have a chance to slip away. To begin, read over lists 11 to 15. Say each word and its meaning aloud.

## ANALOGIES

Circle the one word pair in each list below that expresses the same relationship as the pair in capital letters.

1. **VACILLATE : AMBIVALENCE**
   - (A) disclaim : legitimacy
   - (B) whet : garrulity
   - (C) blaspheme : irreverence
   - (D) delineate : truth
   - (E) indict : suspect

2. **EPHEMERAL : DURATION**
   - (A) scanty : apparel
   - (B) negligible : interest
   - (C) inevitable : weather
   - (D) meager : amount
   - (E) minuscule : portion

3. **SATIRE : IRONY**
   - (A) comedy : tragedy
   - (B) tirade : criticism
   - (C) rhetoric : politics
   - (D) diatribe : speech
   - (E) paucity : emotion

4. **REPUTATION : SLANDER**
   - (A) predilection : favor
   - (B) inquisition : demand
   - (C) sanction : grant
   - (D) indictment : announce
   - (E) communication : garble

5. **SPIRIT : MAGNANIMOUS**
   - (A) criterion : first
   - (B) effort : prodigious
   - (C) edict : quixotic
   - (D) verbosity : redundant
   - (E) dearth : innocuous

## MATCHING
Circle the one synonym or definition that best defines each word in bold type.

1. **defer**
   - (A) pine tree
   - (B) give way to
   - (C) reduce in rank
   - (D) abhor

2. **imply**
   - (A) hint
   - (B) infer
   - (C) layer
   - (D) insult

3. **thwart**
   - (A) confuse
   - (B) harm
   - (C) foil
   - (D) evade

4. **whet**
   - (A) urge
   - (B) illiterate pronoun
   - (C) dampen
   - (D) sharpen

5. **predilection**
   - (A) natural preference
   - (B) hasty decision
   - (C) garbled speech
   - (D) campaign jitters

6. **arduous**
   - (A) complex
   - (B) demanding
   - (C) dubious
   - (D) heartfelt

7. **apocryphal**
   - (A) expeditious
   - (B) fictitious
   - (C) suspicious
   - (D) Aloysius

8. **lethargy**
   - (A) illness
   - (B) slowness
   - (C) paucity
   - (D) langour

9. **explicit**
   - (A) outside the law
   - (B) overextended
   - (C) beyond question
   - (D) aboveboard

10. **redundant**
   - (A) superfluous
   - (B) exceedingly stupid
   - (C) evanescent
   - (D) backward

## FIND THE ODDBALL
In each word group, cross out the oddball, the one unrelated word or phrase.

1. applaud   greet with cheers   acclaim   approve of   announce

2. strengthen   harden   moderate   temper   adjudicate

3. defer to   venerate   revere   admonish   respect

4. speech   brevity   conciseness   succinctness   pithiness

5. garrulous   loquacious   verbose   jargon   gabbiness

6. dirty   appalling   abominable   shockingly awful   heinous

7. worklike   everyday   commonplace   menial   mundane

8. transient   ephemeral   vanishing fast   vapor   evanescent

9. open to question   dubious   suspicious   doubtful   unreal

10. slightly wacko   idealistic   goal-oriented   quixotic

11. dearth   lack   supply   paucity   scarcity   scantiness

12. whiny   querulous   petulant   fretful   adorable

## FILL IN THE BLANKS

From the choices offered below, select the word that best completes the meaning and logic of each sentence. Alter the word as needed to fit the sentence.

| | | | | |
|---|---|---|---|---|
| copious | saturate | prodigal | clamor | pervasive |
| deduce | waive | negligible | vilify | eclectic |
| prodigious | aesthetic | diatribe | conducive | vitriolic |
| capitulate | fluctuate | innocuous | tentative | |

1. "The students who taught this unit are writing the quiz," said the history teacher. "I _____ all control over it."

2. The first question was tough, so I jotted a(n) _____ answer in the margin and decided to come back to it later.

3. Sitting by the window is _____ to thoughts of canoe trips and camping, but not to recalling facts for this test.

4. Getting ready for our yearly winter campout requires careful planning, shopping, and _____ amounts of food because the guys in our group are _____ eaters.

5. We don't let Arturo shop for groceries anymore because he was a _____ spender who bought everything in sight.

6. Although Arturo nearly bankrupted us, we really pigged out on the _____ assortment of groceries he'd purchased.

7. The wilderness of pines and piercingly blue skies in winter appeals to my _____ senses.

8. Last year the temperatures on our trip _____ from below zero at night to the high 30s in the daytime, and there was only a _____ amount of snow.

9. Although we adjusted to the _____ smell of mink that slowly permeated camp, we never _____ where it came from.

10. After a bear raided the food we thought we'd hoisted out of reach, James launched into a furious, _____ speech that _____ all bears. (I'll bet their ears are still burning.)

11. We ordered James to end the _____, and he eventually _____, subsiding into a fairly _____ mumbling as he accused the bears of lying in wait for us each year.

12. With the food mostly gone, our gear _____ with the gamy odor of mink, and our bodies _____ for burgers and hot showers, we packed up and went home to civilization.

**Answers for this review lesson begin on page 205.**

---

undermine • repudiate • enhance • hamper • expedite
• relegate • emulate • squander • rescind • solicit •
emanate • extricate

---

**UNDERMINE** v. *to weaken or destroy bit by bit; to sap the strength of by undercutting*
Nothing *undermines* your image like having a little brother tag along wherever you go. Eddie has been slowly *undermining* my patience too, ever since he learned to walk.

**REPUDIATE** v. *to disown, disclaim, reject, or refuse*
Of course, I always *repudiate* Eddie's determined efforts to follow me. He keeps tracking me like a shadow, however, despite my repeated, stubborn *repudiation*.

**ENHANCE** v. *to make better or more desirable in some way*
One day, I figured I'd *enhance* my chances of losing him if I ducked into a dark alley. Unfortunately, that idea only *enhanced* his interest in following me.

**HAMPER** v. *to get in the way of; to hinder or impede*
How could I *hamper* my dogged little pest? He was certainly *unhampered* by the evil eye I kept giving him.

**EXPEDITE** v. *to smooth or speed up a process; facilitate*
To *expedite* Eddie's departure, I offered him a dollar for ice cream. No way, I was told. As usual, some things just cannot be *expedited*, no matter what you try.

**RELEGATE** v. *to put away or aside; to shift to a less important place; to position by rank*
I thought about *relegating* my brother to a Pests' Dungeon, where he could never annoy me again, but I *relegated* that idea to the back of my mind as I watched his bike suddenly swerve toward the street.

---

**JUG/JUNCT/JOIN = to join or to marry**

**subjugate**—*to subdue or conquer* (**lit.** *"under the yoke"*)
*subjugated* the wildest one
can't *subjugate* the weather

**enjoin**—*to command or order urgently; to forbid or prohibit*
*enjoined* by tradition from participating

Also: **conjugal, conjugate, junction, conjunction, juncture, join, adjoin, rejoinder, injunction**

---

**EMULATE** v. *to try to equal (or even exceed) an example; to imitate* n. **emulation**
He was trying to *emulate* me by popping wheelies as he'd seen me do in our driveway. I yelled, "Cut it out, twerp!" because my example was the wrong one to *emulate*.

**SQUANDER** v. *to use up or spend in an overgenerous or silly way; to dissipate or waste*
Startled by my yell, Eddie rammed his bike into a lamppost, and we *squandered* an hour trying to straighten his wheel. I had planned to *squander* the day in a much more enjoyable way than that, hanging out with my friends.

**RESCIND** v. *to cancel or annul; to repeal, call back*
"I wish I could *rescind* your right to be my brother," I grumbled, sweating over his crumpled bike. It was a mean remark, but I was too angry to *rescind* it at the time.

---

**TORT/TORS = to twist, wring**

**tortuous**—*winding or twisted, like a road; crooked, tricky*
a *tortuous* path up the hillside
a *tortuous* thought process

**extort**—*to get something from a person by using fear or force or unfair power; to obtain by intimidation*
*extorted* the information from him

Also: **retort, distort, torsion, torque, torture, torturous** *(cruel, like torture)*, **tort** *(in law, a wrongful act)*

---

**SOLICIT** v. *to ask for time, money, or moral support; to lure into wrongdoing* adj. **solicitous**, *showing concern*
When I cooled down, I *solicitously* asked if he was okay after his scary adventure. The look I got in reply made me feel as dumb as the guy who tried to *solicit* donations of ice for Eskimos.

**EMANATE** v. *to seep forth (smells or ideas); to emit*
Fists balled at his sides, Eddie glared at me and *emanated* anger. My own fury dwindled as I saw how small and hurt he was. The noise of the streets engulfed us, and cars and buses *emanated* their foul odors as we confronted each other.

**EXTRICATE** v. *to free from an entanglement or awkward spot*
Eventually we got on our bikes, only to stop a few minutes later while Eddie *extricated* his shoelace from his bike gear. As I watched him, I finally accepted the fact that I'd never *extricate* myself from my little brother.

## MEMORY FIX
Once more, write these words down and say each one aloud as you write its synonym or definition.

## FILL IN THE BLANKS
From the list below, select the word that best completes the meaning and logic of each phrase. Alter the words as needed to be grammatically correct.

| | | | |
|---|---|---|---|
| extricate | undermine | subjugate | extort |
| solicitous | relegate | emanate | rescind |
| emulate | expedite | enhance | enjoin |

1. a bylaw that _____ anyone but club members from voting

2. found his authority _____ by their growing criticism

3. put in jail for _____ money from small shopkeepers

4. watching over the sick child with _____ eyes

5. heavenly smell that _____ each spring from honeysuckle

6. old order that was _____ and taken off the books

7. fly will never _____ himself from the spider's web

8. difficult, if not impossible, to _____ Jefferson's achievements

9. carefully printed address will _____ delivery

10. historical habit of the arrogant of _____ others less aggressive

11. _____ that old chair to the basement until it's fixed

12. ready sense of humor that _____ any personality

## RHYME TIME

Choose the correct word from the list of words in this chapter for each blank in this truly corny poetry.

1. Our woeful human tendency to hate,
   I would like to and I do _____!

2. If I tell you not to _____,
   that means don't apply a damper
   to my one essential whim.
   For I won't be _____
   to the group whose lives are fated
   to be meaningless or grim.

3. I'll _____ my invitation to the dance,

   Unless you _____ the look of those pants!

4. Will and Orville were told not to _____

   Their time by aiming up yonder.

   But they wanted to fly,

   So they gave it a try.

   Of the outcome, we couldn't be fonder.

5. I'm obliged to report

   That your attempt to _____

   A confession from this dope

   Is a prospect without hope.

## MATCHING

Match the words in column A with their synonyms or definitions in column B and write them down in the space provided.

|  | A | B |
|---|---|---|
| _____ | 1. expedite | tortuous |
| _____ | 2. dissipate | weaken gradually |
| _____ | 3. solicit | repeal |
| _____ | 4. hinder | forbid |
| _____ | 5. undermine | try to equal |
| _____ | 6. emanate | squander |
| _____ | 7. enjoin | ask for |
| _____ | 8. emulate | hamper |
| _____ | 9. twisted | facilitate |
| _____ | 10. rescind | seep out |

**Answers for this chapter begin on page 205.**

# AN ESTEEMED ASSORTMENT

---

**esteem • disparity • catharsis • anomaly • censure • antithesis • fallacy • indolence • fledgling • hindrance • clemency • jeopardy**

---

**ESTEEM** n. *high opinion of one's worth or character* v. **esteem, to value extremely**
Because the British are known to *esteem* royalty, English diarist Samuel Pepys (pronounced "peeps") jokingly wrote this about King Charles II: "Methought it lessened my *esteem* of a king, that he should not be able to command the rain."

**DISPARITY** n. *difference in type, quality, or quantity* adj. **disparate**
Although we think there's a *disparity* between passion and reason, the English poet John Donne blended them in his poetry. After all, the perceived *disparity* between love and hate is believed to be two sides of one coin.

**CATHARSIS** n. *a cleansing or purging that releases emotions* adj. **cathartic**
A funeral is meant to be a *cathartic* event that allows us to vent our grief openly and fully so that it is no longer a burden. Tears are one obvious form of *catharsis*, of course.

**ANOMALY** n. *something different from the norm; irregularity or paradox* adj. **anomalous**
As a night owl, I'm an *anomaly* in a family of early risers who turn into pumpkins at 10 p.m. An irregularity of any kind usually sticks out, like the *anomalous* black sheep.

**CENSURE** n. *stern or official condemnation* v. **censure**
"No man can justly *censure* or condemn another," wrote the seventeenth-century English physician Sir Thomas Browne, "because indeed no man truly knows another." Yes, but what would the media do without *censure*?

---

**GREG = crowd, flock, group**

**gregarious**—*social and convivial; fond of groups*
     her bubbly, *gregarious* personality
     the *gregarious* elephant

**egregious**—*painfully noticeable; flagrant; outstandingly bad*
     *egregious* error
     disciplined the child's *egregious* behavior

Also: **congregate, congregation, aggregate, segregate**

---

**ANTITHESIS** n. *a direct opposite* adj. **antithetical**
The world has lots of "near opposites," but truly *antithetical* things are rare. War is the *antithesis* of peace, day the *antithesis* of night, and good the *antithesis* of evil.

**FALLACY** n. *incorrect idea; wrong assumption; an error* adj. **fallacious**
The idea behind the "pathetic *fallacy*" is that when you're under severe emotional strain, you're easy prey to *fallacious* impressions. For example, it's a *fallacy* to believe that nature rejoices along with you, just because you are happy.

**INDOLENCE** n. *supreme laziness or idleness; sloth*
Mom's last vacation was a study in *indolence*, as she put it. "I'm majoring in sloth this week, and I refuse to even move in that direction," she said, waving one *indolent* hand toward the kitchen.

---

**NOV/NEO = new**

**novel**—*new or original*
**innovate**—*to do something new*
     a *novel* idea
     *novel* solution
     a highly *innovative* plan

**neophyte**—*novice, beginner, tyro, newcomer, proselyte*
     a *neophyte* on the court
     fresh ideas from our *neophyte*

Also: **novelty, novice, novitiate, renovate, neon, neonatal, neologism**

---

**FLEDGLING** n. *a young bird with new flight feathers; an untested beginner; novice*
Every field has its *fledglings*—people who have the knowledge or equipment for a job but haven't yet proved themselves. Most *fledglings* are marked by an appealing enthusiasm.

**HINDRANCE** n. *an obstacle, impediment; something in the way*
v. **hinder**, *to impede*
At leaf-raking time, Dude becomes a real *hindrance*. He darts wildly into our tidy leaf piles, scattering leaves everywhere and *hindering* the entire project of fall cleanup.

**CLEMENCY** n. *lenience or moderation in punishment; mercy* adj. **clement**, *mild (weather); merciful*
In *The Merchant of Venice*, Portia asks that justice be tempered with *clemency* for Antonio, who owes Shylock a pound of flesh. That famous soliloquy seeking a *clement* judgment begins, ''The quality of mercy is not strain'd, It droppeth as the gentle rain from heaven. . . .''

**JEOPARDY** n. *an exposure to or possibility of danger*
*Jeopardy* began as the Latin phrase *jocus partitus*, tied game, then became French, *jeu parti*, meaning that the game's outcome was uncertain. Now when people are in *jeopardy* they are at risk or even in serious danger—except on the program of that name, which is still a game.

## MEMORY FIX
Quick, take out a piece of paper and write down each of these new words along with a definition.

## TRUE OR FALSE
Read each sentence to see how the words in this chapter are being used. Then mark **T** (true) or **F** (false) beside each.

**1.** Any business is managed best by a *neophyte*. _____

**2.** Acquiring knowledge helps to build *self-esteem*. _____

**3.** Repeated *censure* destroys self-esteem. _____

**4.** Rage is the *antithesis* of anger. _____

5. A stew is typically made from *disparate* ingredients. _____

6. There are noticeable *disparities* between identical twins.

   _____

7. The most prized assistant is an *indolent* one. _____

8. It's tough to hide an *anomaly* in the herd. Likewise, an *anomaly* in the herd had better have a tough hide. _____

9. When sad or depressed, spending time with comics Robin Williams and Billy Crystal might be very *cathartic*. _____

10. Thinking that I'll be a good diver because I'm a good swimmer is probably *fallacious* reasoning. _____

## FIND THE ODDBALL

In each word group below, cross out the oddball, the one unrelated word or phrase.

1. regard   value   prize   outlook   esteem

2. honor   merciful   forgiving   lenient   indulgent

3. strong disapproval   urgency   condemnation   censure

4. symbiosis   antonymous pair   opposition   antithesis

5. master   tyro   neophyte   novice   fledgling   proselyte

6. original   different   novel   fresh   hackneyed

7. sociable   convivial   aloof   social   gregarious

## MATCHING

Find two synonyms or phrases in column B that explain each word in column A.

|  | **A** | **B** |
|---|---|---|
| _____ | 1. indolence | sociable |
| _____ |  | obstacle |
| _____ | 2. clemency | paradox |
| _____ |  | a purging |
| _____ | 3. catharsis | lenience |
| _____ |  | error |
| _____ | 4.fallacy | neophyte |
| _____ |  | idleness |
| _____ | 5. hindrance | a cleansing |
| _____ |  | convivial |
| _____ | 6. anomaly | mercy |
| _____ |  | flagrant |
| _____ | 7. fledgling | sloth |
| _____ |  | irregularity |
| _____ | 8. gregarious | outstandingly bad |
| _____ |  | novice |
| _____ | 9. novel | wrong assumption |
| _____ |  | original |
| _____ | 10. egregious | impediment |
| _____ |  | new |

**Answers for this chapter begin on page 206.**

---

benign • blithe • elation • appease • jocular •
effervescent • extol • placid • ameliorate • serene •
frivolous • assuage

---

**BENIGN** adj. *gentle, gracious, kind; benevolent in outlook; mild or favorable, not malignant*
The dermatologist smiled *benignly* and urged me to relax. "The results of the biopsies show that the moles we removed from your hand were *benign*, not malignant, Ted."

**BLITHE** adj. *cheerful, lighthearted; or, casual or heedless*
A while back, I strolled in around 2 a.m. from a party, whistling *blithely*, only to meet my parents in the kitchen. They were waiting up for me, and the look on their faces was anything but *blithe*.

**ELATION** n. *exultation; high spirits* v. **elate**
When I saw those furious faces, my *elation* quickly faded, and I felt myself turning red. I have turned red other times, when I was exercising hard or *elated* over something, but this was a different red altogether.

**APPEASE** v. *to quiet, calm, allay; to pacify or conciliate (refers to people or emotions, not conditions)*
I knew it was time to *appease* the folks, and in a hurry. I choose the truth because it was my only hope, as I saw it, of *appeasing* their anger.

**JOCULAR** adj. *jolly, fond of joking (L. joc = joke);* also, **jocose** *and* **jocund** = *merry, witty*
My folks are *jocular* people. Dad has even called home in the middle of the day to relate some *jocose* remark from a friend at work.

**EFFERVESCENT** adj. *bubbling with high spirits; exhilarated* v. **to effervesce** n. **effervescence**
Mom's usually an *effervescent* person, bubbling over with enthusiasm about one thing or another. It's hard to resist anybody whose spirit *effervesces* like that.

> **AM = to love; friend**
>
> amiable—*easy to get along with; friendly and good-natured*
> a spaniel's gentle, *amiable* nature
> an *amiable* settlement
>
> amity—*friendship and good-will; harmony*
> a nation known for *amity*
> the natural *amity* of old friends
>
> Also: **amicable, enamored, amorous, amatory, amateur, paramour**

## EXTOL v. *to "sing" the praises of; glorify, praise highly*

I don't usually *extol* the virtues of my parents, but when I meet other kids' folks, I know I am luckier than most. Of course, my folks *extol* their terrific kids all the time, but you expect that of parents.

## PLACID v. *calm in nature, not easily ruffled; quiet, serene*

I am quieter than my parents, not *placid* exactly, but not always joking around either. My friend Greg is so *placid* that people often wonder if he's asleep.

## AMELIORATE v. *to improve or better (a condition)*

Anyway, to return to the night of the Big Bad Late Party, I was able to *ameliorate* the whole sticky situation by explaining to my folks that I'd met the perfect woman. Telling the truth doesn't always *ameliorate* a problem, but it's amazing how it has repeatedly helped me.

> **PATH/PAS = feeling, suffering, disease**
>
> apathy—*lack of feeling or interest; impassiveness; indifference*
> an *apathetic* nod
> unfortunate *apathy* toward the poor
>
> dispassionate—*fair; not affected by strong feeling*
> a *dispassionate* opinion
> a carefully *dispassionate* review
>
> Also: **sympathy, empathy, antipathy, pathos, pathetic, sociopath, passion, compassion, impassive, pathology**

**SERENE** adj. *extremely quiet, calm, and peaceful*
As I explained about meeting Beth, I saw Mom lean back against the kitchen wall and relax, gradually becoming more *serene*. She wasn't totally calm, not Mrs. *Serenity*-of-the-year or anything, but she was definitely calmer.

**FRIVOLOUS** adj. *not serious; inappropriately high-spirited; foolishly self-indulgent* n. **frivolity**
When I finished talking, Dad said, "Thanks, Ted. I wasn't in the mood for any *frivolous* excuses." I smiled, because at two in the morning he has never been in the mood for anything, let alone something *frivolous*!

**ASSUAGE** v. *to ease or relieve something that hurts or is worrisome; to quiet, pacify; to appease*
So that's my Parent-Management Tip of the Week, I guess: The best way to *assuage* your folks' worries is to tell them what really happened. *Assuaging* someone's fears isn't always this easy, of course, because sometimes truth is painful.

## MEMORY FIX
Write each of these new words now, along with a synonym or definition for each. It helps to say them aloud as you write.

## FIND THE SYNONYMS
From the word choices offered below, select the missing synonym for each numbered word group.

> amiable   benign   amity   apathetic   dispassionate
> jocular   elated   serene   frivolity   effervescent

1. joyous silliness   costly trifle   unseemly humor
   _____

2. pleasant   easygoing   friendly   amicable _____

3. high-spirited   overjoyed   filled with pleasure
   _____

4. emotionless   unaffected by feelings _____

5. revealing no emotion   impassive _____

6. bubbling with enthusiasm   exhilarated _____

7. placid   calm   quiet   peaceful   unflappable

_____

8. benevolent   kind   favorable   gentle _____

9. friendship   accord   harmonious relations _____

10. jocose   lighthearted   humorous   jocund _____

## FILL IN THE BLANKS

Select the new word in this chapter that best completes the meaning and logic of each phrase. Remember to use the correct form of the word.

1. benefited from the _____ influence of the monks

2. a travelogue that _____ the many virtues of Spain

3. a nature so serene, so eternally _____, that I wondered if she had any passion at all

4. with more _____ than a bottle of soda pop

5. a serious attempt to _____ the deteriorating state of the building

6. a(n) _____ but enjoyable way to blow all of my allowance

7. amusing Noel Coward play, _____ *Spirit*, about a humorous, cheerful ghost

8. thoughtful talk that attempted to _____ our fears about the upcoming changes

9. announcing his promotion with obvious _____

10. a(n) _____ note meant to _____ Grandma after we'd made a mess in her yard

## FIND THE ANTONYMS
Match up the opposites by writing them on the correct lines.

| | | |
|---|---|---|
| _____ | 1. elated | dispassionate |
| _____ | 2. impassive | censure |
| _____ | 3. appease | overwrought |
| _____ | 4. passionate | downcast |
| _____ | 5. extol | irritate |
| _____ | 6. sensible | effervescent |
| _____ | 7. placid | frivolous |

**Answers for this chapter begin on page 206.**

# LIST 19
# MIGHTY OBVIOUS OPPOSITES

---

partial/impartial • potent/impotent • inflate/deflate •
famous/infamous • savory/unsavory • tangible/
intangible • auspicious/inauspicious • discriminate/
indiscriminate • consent/dissent • neutral/biased

---

**PARTIAL** adj. *biased or even strongly disposed toward; or,
referring to a portion of a whole*
**IMPARTIAL** adj. *unbiased, not prejudiced; fair, evenhanded*
At election time, journalists need to be *impartial* in their coverage of all
candidates. Even if they're *partial* to one, they should avoid showing
that *partiality* in print.

**POTENT** adj. *strong, powerful; effective (as "a potent remedy")*
**IMPOTENT** adj. *lacking effectiveness; weak, lacking strength*
Age proves to us that words are *potent* weapons. As kids we chanted,
"Sticks and stones my break my bones, but words will never harm me."
Yet we suspected way back then that words were far from *impotent*.

**INFLATE** v. *to blow or puff up, either literally or figuratively; to
expand or enlarge, sometimes unwisely*
**DEFLATE** v. *to let the air out of, thereby reducing in size, either
a tire or someone's ego*
As we *inflated* balloons to celebrate Greg's victory as class president, I
could see his ego *inflating*, too. "Hey, buddy," I said, to *deflate* him a bit
before he got too obnoxious, "there's a zit on your nose."

**FAMOUS** adj. *widely known; outstanding, noted, excellent* adv.
**famously**, *very or extremely*
**INFAMOUS** adj. *of exceedingly bad repute; disgraceful* n. **infamy**
Our family has a set of widely diverse twins, one *famous* for his
generosity, the other *infamous* for deceiving everyone he meets. That
kind of *infamy* I can live without!

---

**CRAC/CRAT = to rule**

**autocrat**—*one who makes and executes the laws; dictator*
    iron rule of the *autocrat*
    a clearly *autocratic* decision

**aristocracy**—*a privileged class; certain well-qualified people; an upper class of hereditary nobility*
    the local *aristocracy*
    fine, *aristocratic* bearing

Also: **democrat, democracy, theocracy, plutocracy, aristocrat**

---

**SAVORY** adj. *very tasty, palatable; referring to a good reputation; edifying or mind-pleasing*
**UNSAVORY** adj. *smelling or tasting bad; morally repugnant or disgusting; distasteful*
In merrie olde England, a meat *savory* was a spiced meat dish served as an appetizer. Now, because the word's meaning has grown, you can be a person with a *savory* reputation (excellent) who enjoys *savory* foods (tasty) while writing a collection of *savory* essays (mind-pleasing). Of course, anything *unsavory* is highly suspect, like that fellow who has an *unsavory* reputation.

---

**DEM = people**

**demagogue**—*false leader who tells people what they want to hear, using popular prejudices to win approval*
    the latest *demagogue* in office
    empty talk of a *demagogue*

**pandemic**—*throughout an entire* (pan) *population* (dem)
    *pandemic* illness
    a tendency to become *pandemic*

Also: **epidemic, democrat, democracy, endemic, demographics**

**TANGIBLE** adj. *real, concrete, able to be touched (palpable); perceptible*
**INTANGIBLE** adj. *not concrete; impalpable yet real, such as cheerfulness*
Labeled a "decade of greed," the '80s were a time when people eagerly acquired impressive *tangible* property, such as luxury cars and huge houses. Perhaps the new century will see an emphasis on *intangible* assets, like concern for others.

**AUSPICIOUS** adj. *highly favorable; propitious* n. auspice, *a prophetic sign*
**INAUSPICIOUS** adj. *unfavorable; foreboding ill*
The Roman *auspex* divined the future by studying the flight and feeding patterns of birds. If the *auspices* were *auspicious*, he advised a ruler to act confidently. *Inauspicious* signs foretold trouble. When my car's engine overheated, I knew that was a very *inauspicious* sign.

**DISCRIMINATE** v. *to notice differences, distinguish clearly between objects or choices; to treat differently*
**INDISCRIMINATE** adj. *at random, without discrimination; haphazard*
I can easily *discriminate* among various pizzas and tell you which is best and why. I would never grab any old piece of pizza, making a totally *indiscriminate* choice, because pizza is important to me.

**CONSENT** n. *agreement; acceptance* v. consent, *to agree to*
**DISSENT** n. *disagreement* v. dissent, *to disagree*
Class presidents obtained the *consent* of each class before a large donated sum was spent on band uniforms and equipment. Of course, some sports fans *dissented*, but they were overruled for once.

**NEUTRAL** adj. *without bias or prejudice; neither for nor against*
**BIASED** adj. *prejudiced; having a distinct feeling one way or another*
Modern Sweden is a *neutral* country that has not taken sides in a war or funded a "war chest" like the United States. The U.S., *biased* in favor of democracy, has spent billions promoting that method of government and defending it.

## MEMORY FIX
This time, write down only the words you DO NOT KNOW and their meanings. Say these words aloud as you write them.

## WORDS IN CONTEXT
Write the meaning of each italicized word on the line provided.

1. the most *unsavory* concoction I ever saw

   _____

2. an *inflated* idea of his own importance

   _____

3. the immensity of the problem made her feel totally *impotent*

   _____

4. always *partial* to something chocolate

   _____

5. the *intangible* reward of their gratitude

   _____

6. his A+ was an *auspicious* beginning for the year

   _____

7. giving out candy with an *indiscriminate* hand

   _____

8. Clay's ability to turn *dissent* into compromise

   _____

9. choose consensus rather than the dictates of an *autocrat*

   _____

10. a member of the feline *aristocracy*, unlike our Meatloaf

    _____

## TRUE OR FALSE

Read each sentence to see how the words in this chapter are being used. Then mark **T** (true) or **F** (false) beside each.

1. A *demagogue* needs both candor and sincerity. _____

2. Onc rcason to select jurors with care is to eliminate *biased* individuals and choose *impartial* ones. _____

3. Vampires scoff at *potent* spells against them. _____

4. Fans hang around stage doors hoping for a glimpse of the most *infamous* stars. _____

5. I'd be eager to taste a *savory* dish offered as *tangible* proof of your culinary skills. _____

6. Mozart's talent was so great that it is sometimes difficult to *discriminate* between early works and later ones. _____

7. The various cold viruses are properly termed *pandemic*. _____

8. Blue skies are an *inauspicious* omen in the morning. _____

9. *Deflated* team spirits can translate into a quick loss of yardage on the football field. _____

10. The more you know about a subject, the harder it may be to remain totally *neutral*. _____

**Answers for this chapter begin on page 206.**

# LIST 20

# COMPLIMENT? NOT!

---

**didactic • fickle • gullible • insipid • petty • incorrigible • officious • pompous • inane • willful • tedious • wanton**

---

**DIDACTIC** adj. *instructive, designed to teach; morally "preachy"; pedantic*
The word *didactic* originated in Greece and meant "apt in teaching." Today, anything described as *didactic* is apt to be preachy, dull, or both.

**FICKLE** adj. *changeable, inconstant, irresolute; not steadfast*
The faithless behavior of a *fickle* lover is the subject of the old country-western favorite, "Your Cheatin' Heart." One sex is always accusing the other of being *fickle*.

**GULLIBLE** adj. *easily fooled; naive, ingenuous, innocent*
A *gullible* person swallows whatever you tell him, maybe down his gullet? And a *gull* is a fool or dupe who's easily decieved. Remember that *gullible* fellow who thought he was buying the Brooklyn Bridge for $24?

**INSIPID** adj. *lacking flavor, zip, or interest; dull, flat*
To French novelist Anatole France, "A tale without love is like beef without mustard: *insipid*." (What a thoroughly French analogy.) *Mais oui*, the world would be an infinitely more *insipid* place without love and mustard.

**PETTY** adj. *of minor importance; small-minded*
Near the end of *Macbeth*, King Macbeth says, "Tomorrow, and tomorrow, and tomorrow/Creeps in this *petty* pace from day to day," beginning a world-famous soliloquy. In modern use, anything *petty* is usually small-minded in nature.

**INCORRIGIBLE** adj. *extremely difficult to manage or control; delinquent, recalcitrant*
Having lived with two *incorrigible* pets, I understand this word. Our own *incorrigible* cat sleeps in the clothes dryer but doesn't enjoy tumbling about on high heat.

---

### DOG/DOX = opinion, praise

**dogmatic**—*stubbornly opinionated; dictatorial; doctrinaire*
> the autocrat's *dogmatic* approach
> unpopular *dogmatic* style

**orthodox**—*according to traditional teaching or established religious doctrine; "by the book"*
> in an *orthodox* manner
> comfortable, *orthodox* presentation

Also: **dogma, doxology, paradox, heterodox**

---

**OFFICIOUS** adj. *self-important and meddlesome; interfering; impertinent*
An *officious* person is a "buttinski"; you know the type. As writer Ivan Krylov put it, "Heaven save you from a foolish friend; the too *officious* fool is worse than any foe."

**POMPOUS** adj. *puffed up with self-importance; arrogant*
Just as unpopular as the "officious fool" is the "*pompous* ass"—someone dying to impress you with his importance or knowledge. Unfortunately, one afflicted with *pomposity* is all too often known for verbosity as well.

**INANE** adj. *witless, empty, insipid, "dopey"*
The best *inane* giggle in show business belonged to Butterfly McQueen, who played the part of a witless young girl in *Gone With the Wind*. Only a fine actress like Ms. McQueen could have created such a believably *inane* yet lovable character.

---

### DOC/DACT = to teach

**docile**—*easily controlled or taught; compliant, tractable, amenable, obedient*
> a *docile* breed of cows
> a sweet, *docile* child

**indoctrinate**—*to teach the basics; teach a specific point of view*
> *indoctrinated* by church leaders
> *indoctrinate* new members

Also: **doctor, doctrine, doctrinaire, didactic**

---

**WILLFUL** adj. *headstrong; stubbornly self-willed; unruly*
Incorrigible pets like ours are *willful* ones, determined to do what they want just like young children. Once when Eddie didn't get his way, he ground a banana into our new rug, a *willful* act that got him into a lot of trouble.

**TEDIOUS** adj. *tiresome, boring; seeming too long or dull*
Anatole France, a most quotable satirist, wrote that "historical books which contain no lies are extremely *tedious*." History is fascinating if you like it, of course, and only *tedious* if you don't.

**WANTON** adj. *arousing sexual desire; lacking human kindness (as in "wanton cruelty"); malicious; unchecked (as in "a wanton growth of weeds")*
Behind all the meanings of *wanton* is the idea of uncontrolled behavior. Not all things need control, of course, such as wildflowers that grow on the hillsides in *wanton* profusion.

## MEMORY FIX
As with the last list, write down only the words you don't know or are unsure about. As you note their meanings, say each word aloud.

## SUBSTITUTION
Replace each italicized word or phrase with the correct new word from this chapter.

1.  The salesman delivered a *teaching* talk that was surprisingly interesting and convincing. _____

2.  "I guess I'm sort of *easily deceived*," my cousin Sara confessed later, hiding her latest purchase behind her back.

    _____

3.  "Maybe I'm even *impossible to control*," she went on miserably, "because I always fall for a good spiel." _____

4.  I shrugged and gave her an *empty, silly* smile, but her *loose and uncontrolled* purchases were getting on my nerves.

    _____   _____

5. "Well," I harrumphed, "I don't mean to be *tiresome or boring*, but shouldn't you quit this?" _____

6. Sara gave me a smile that was anything but *obedient* and said, "You don't need to act so *self-important*!"

   _____   _____

7. I mumbled, "Sorry. I hate people who are *meddlesome and interfering*." _____

8. "That's better," she replied. "It's not like you to be *small-minded*, either, so let's forget it." _____

9. "Sure. Just put that food grinder away with all the others," I said, not caring that I sounded *dictatorial*. _____

10. Defeated, she gave me a(n) *zestless* smile. "Ah, clever cousin. How did you know it was another food grinder?"

    _____

## MATCHING
From the list below, find two synonyms for each numbered word and write them in on the correct lines.

| | | | | |
|---|---|---|---|---|
| pedantic | unchecked | naive | established | delinquent |
| inconstant | flavorless | preachy | tractable | ingenuous |
| witless | recalcitrant | insipid | traditional | inhumane |
| compliant | changeable | dull | interfering | impertinent |

1. fickle _____   _____

2. gullible _____   _____

3. insipid _____   _____

4. didactic _____   _____

5. incorrigible _____   _____

6. inane _____   _____

7. wanton _____   _____

8. orthodox _____   _____

9. docile _____   _____

10. officious _____   _____

## FIND THE ODDBALL

In each word group, cross out the oddball, the one unrelated word or phrase.

1. mean-spirited   ugly   unimportant   minor   petty

2. unsavory   self-important   arrogant   pompous   puffed-up

3. unruly   willful   stubbornly determined   headstrong   biased

4. theoretical   traditional   orthodox   established

5. instruct   train   indoctrinate   teach a doctrine   moderate

6. fickle   doctrinaire   dogmatic   opinionated   dictatorial

**Answers for this chapter begin on page 207.**

# LISTS 16–20 REVIEW

Just in case a few words from lists 16 through 20 have gone astray, it's time to review. Read those lists again, then you can whip through these few reminder-type exercises.

## ANALOGIES

Circle the one word pair in each list below that expresses the same relationship as the pair in capital letters.

1. **REASONING : FALLACIOUS**
   (A) logic : dispassionate
   (B) behavior : docile
   (C) ruling : orthodox
   (D) judgment : biased
   (E) demeanor : amiable

2. **INFAMY : CENSURE**
   (A) studies : indoctrinate
   (B) pettiness : extricate
   (C) virtue : extol
   (D) amity : savor
   (E) novelty : enjoin

3. **PLEASANT : JOCULAR**
   (A) insipid : inane
   (B) famous : cultured
   (C) serene : placid
   (D) clement : mild
   (E) contented : blithe

4. **DEMAGOGUE : SINCERITY**
   (A) neophyte : experience
   (B) feline : indolence
   (C) aristocracy : dogma
   (D) conflict : jeopardy
   (E) autocrat : pomposity

5. **EFFERVESCENT : ELATION**
   (A) overjoyed : emulation
   (B) deflated : repudiation
   (C) incorrigible : apathy
   (D) indecision : clemency
   (E) impassive : discrimination

6. **CONFIDENCE : UNDERMINE**
   (A) capital : squander
   (B) fears : assuage
   (C) donation : solicit
   (D) consent : extort
   (E) embankment : erode

## MATCHING ANTONYMS

Match the antonyms by writing the correct opposite beside each numbered word.

| | |
|---|---|
| _____ | 1. intangible   ominous, foreboding |
| _____ | 2. officious   similarity |
| _____ | 3. wanton   ineffective |
| _____ | 4. expedite   agreement |
| _____ | 5. ameliorate   engrossing, absorbing |
| _____ | 6. auspicious   disgrace |
| _____ | 7. dissent   implicate |
| _____ | 8. tedious   concrete |
| _____ | 9. potent   aggravate |
| _____ | 10. esteem   humble |
| _____ | 11. disparity   carefully controlled |
| _____ | 12. extricate   hinder |

## FIND THOSE SYNONYMS

On the lines provided, write the two best synonyms from this list of words to complete each numbered word group.

| | | | | |
|---|---|---|---|---|
| repeal | enjoin | unfeeling | impede | assuage |
| vacillating | hinder | inconstant | amicable | insipid |
| conciliate | novice | call back | crooked | empty |
| command | tortuous | gregarious | beginner | apathetic |

1. hamper _____ obstruct _____

2. rescind _____ annul _____

3. _____ forbid _____ prohibit

4. _____ twisted _____ winding

5. fledgling _____ tyro _____

6. sociable _____ convivial _____

7. _____ fickle _____ changeable

8. _____ appease _____ pacify

9. impassive _____ indifferent

_____

10. inane _____ silly _____

## GOOD WORDS GET AROUND

From the words listed below, fill in the blanks in these quotations.

> alleviates  squander  petty       placid
> frivolous   dogmatic  undermining  impartial

1. "To waste, to destroy our natural resources, to skin and exhaust
   the land instead of using it so as to increase its usefulness, will
   result in _____ in the days of our children the
   very prosperity which we ought by right to hand down to them
   amplified and developed."
   —Theodore Roosevelt, address to Congress, 1907

2. "Pale Death with _____ tread beats at the poor
   man's cottage door and at the palace of kings."
   —Horace, Roman poet and satirist

3. "Dost thou love life? Then do not _____ time;
   for that's the stuff life is made of."
   —Benjamin Franklin, *Poor Richard's Almanack*

4. "There is a strange charm in the thoughts of a good legacy . . .
   which wondrously _____ the sorrow that men
   would otherwise feel for the death of friends."
   —Miguel Cervantes, *Don Quixote*

5. "I think I could turn and live with animals, they are so
   _____ and self-contained."
   —Walt Whitman, *Song of Myself*

6. "One who is serious all day will never have a good time, while
   one who is _____ all day will never establish a
   household."
   —Ancient Egyptian maxim

7. "When people are least sure, they are often most
   _____." (Look for irony here.)
   —John Kenneth Galbraith, American economist

8. "Why, man, he [Caesar] doth bestride the narrow world
   Like a Colossus; and we _____ men
   Walk under his huge legs, and peep about
   To find ourselves dishonourable graves."
   —Shakespeare, *Julius Caesar*

**Answers for this review lesson begin on page 207.**

# AH, THE PRUDENT PURITANS

---

**frugal** • **exemplary** • **diligent** • **prudent** • **scrupulous** • **parochial** • **pious** • **discreet** • **thrifty** • **solemn** • **pragmatic** • **steadfast**

---

**FRUGAL** adj. *careful in using resources; sparing, thrifty*
Since I got my car, which eats cash, I've had to be *frugal* in all my spending. I can't keep this money-guzzler going unless *frugality* is my motto from now on.

**EXEMPLARY** adj. *serving as a model; commendable*
I had an *exemplary* month recently—didn't buy any extras—but did the car reward me with *exemplary* behavior? Hardly. It blew its head gasket.

**DILIGENT** adj. *showing painstaking care and attention*
I'll have to slave *diligently* for months to pay off this repair, and I bet it was my fault. The engine overheated because I wasn't *diligent* about keeping the radiator full.

**PRUDENT** adj. *shrewd and careful in managing things; wise; discreet, circumspect; also, frugal*
Luckily I know a *prudent* auto mechanic, Raoul, who owns a small local garage. Raoul hires only the best repairmen and *prudently* stocks rebuilt parts as well.

**SCRUPULOUS** adj. *showing painstaking care; extremely attentive to detail or to morality*
"A real mechanic," says Raoul, "pays *scrupulous* attention to details. I examine every connection, every hose, *scrupulously*, because overlooking even one thing can be disastrous."

**PAROCHIAL** adj. *of narrow, limited scope; provincial; referring to a church parish*
In addition to his ownership of the garage, Raoul has a *parochial* job as a lay priest. Until I got to know him, I had a totally uninformed and *parochial* view of his religion.

---

**GEN = kind, race, birth, cause**

congenial—*having kindred tastes; like-minded; sociable*
    a pleasant, *congenial* fellow
    having a *congenial* outlook

generic—*universal, general; referring to a group or class*
    a bottle of *generic* aspirin
    a *generic* form of gelatin

Also: **ingenuous** *(naive)*, **engender** *(foster, begin)*, **gentleman**,
**disingenuous** *(faking honesty)*, **homogeneous** (The **gen** words
love to appear on SATs.)

---

**PIOUS** adj. *noticeably religious, sometimes to the point of
hypocrisy; or, honestly religious and devoted* n. **piety**
Even if he is a lay priest, Raoul doesn't go around making *pious*
comments about religion all the time. His *piety* is real, not phony;
anyone can tell how sincere he is.

**DISCREET** adj. *showing good sense (prudence) in behavior;
circumspect; modest (as in "discreet of speech")* n. **discretion**
Dad and I had one of those *discreet*, father-son talks last night, away from
the rest of the family. Of course, any kid should use some *discretion*
when he's talking to a parent, but Dad and I have always been pretty
open with each other.

---

**CRED = to believe**

credible—*believable, trustworthy; worthy of being believed*
    a *credible* witness
    would never question his *credibility*

credulous—*willing to believe almost anything; gullible*
    a young, *credulous* person
    a *credulous* dog, easily fooled

Also: **incredible** *(amazing)*, **incredulous** *(unbelieving)*, **credit**,
**creditable**, **discredit**, **credentials**

---

**THRIFTY** adj. *extremely careful with money; provident, sparing, frugal* n. **thrift**
"You'll have to be extra *thrifty*," Dad said, "to pay off a repair bill that size. I've always been a rather *thrifty* fellow myself, so I can afford to lend you money at no interest—how's that?"

**SOLEMN** adj. *extremely serious; sober, sedate*
I'd already worked out a payment schedule with Raoul, so I made Dad a *solemn* promise that he didn't have to worry about me and my car. "I admire the way you're handling this, Ted," Dad said, pretty *solemn* himself.

**PRAGMATIC** adj. *practical, not idealistic; sensible* n. **pragmatist (person) and pragmatism**
I thought I'd made a normal, *pragmatic* arrangement to pay my bill, so I was surprised by Dad's praise. Now that I own a car that eats money, I'm forced to operate in a more *pragmatic*, thoughtful way.

**STEADFAST** adj. *not apt to change; steady, faithful, loyal*
My friend Greg really fits the word *steadfast*, even if it sounds old-fashioned. In fact, he's such a *steadfast* friend that he's paying part of my repair bill, because he always depends on me for his transportation.

## MEMORY FIX
On a separate piece of paper, just like before, write down each word in this list along with a definition and say each one aloud.

## FILL IN THE BLANKS
Select the new word from this chapter that best completes the meaning and logic of each sentence. Alter the form of the word as needed for sense.

1. She's so _____ she'd believe anything you tell her.

2. Jana needs to give _____ attention to that experiment so that each chemical is added at the right time.

3. _____ is a perfect antonym of fickle.

4. The prodigal spender is the antithesis of the
   _____ soul who lives a life based on
   _____.

5. A crazy idealist like Don Quixote is clearly not a
   _____.

6. Little Lord Fauntleroy and Miss Goody Two-Shoes were known for
   their _____ conduct.

7. Turn six words from this lesson into nouns, and you have six
   virtues esteemed by the Puritans: _____,
   _____, _____,
   _____, _____, and
   _____.

8. The Puritanical outlook was unfortunately _____,
   an irony when you consider that they settled the colonies to
   escape prejudice.

9. The Puritans are always portrayed as a somber lot, known for
   their _____ of manner and
   _____ clothing to match.

10. It took only a brief time to establish the _____ of
    _____ drugs, which are the same as the name
    brands but without the big price tag.

## ADD THE SYNONYMS

From this chapter's word list, definitions, and synonyms, complete each
numbered word group.

1. thrifty _____ prudent _____

2. circumspect _____ discreet

3. of a church parish _____ provincial

4.  praiseworthy commendable _____ acting as a
    model

5.  attentive to detail _____ showing painstaking care

6.  loyal _____ steady _____

7.  like-minded _____ sociable

    _____

## TRUE OR FALSE

Read the sentences below and then mark **T** (true) or **F** (false) for each.

1.  The most effective liar is a wholly *credible* one. _____

2.  You might as well dismiss an accountant who's been accused of
    *scrupulousness*. _____

3.  The name THRIFT DRUG encourages you to think it will be a
    *prudent* place to shop. _____

4.  Puritans would have preferred a little levity or frivolity in church
    compared to all that *solemnity* they endured. _____

5.  Say that a president is a *pragmatist* and he's doomed. _____

6.  The older you get, the more *credulous* you're apt to be. _____

7.  Because *generic* products don't pay for advertising, they can be
    sold at lower costs. _____

8.  The best college roommate would be a *congenial* person. _____

**Answers for this chapter begin on page 208.**

clairvoyant • chimera • eccentric • karma • enigma •
vicarious • hypothetical • cryptic • esoteric • oblivious
• utopia • elusive

**CLAIRVOYANT** n. *one who perceives far more than the normal five senses would explain; a seer* adj. **extraordinarily perceptive** n. **clairvoyance**

In the days before science took hold, people turned to a *clairvoyant* for explanations of the inexplicable. In the twentieth century, only those who study paranormal psychology are comfortable with the possibility of true *clairvoyance* in humans.

**CHIMERA (ki-'mir-e)** n. *a Greek mythic being with a lion's head, goat's body, and a serpent's tail* adj. **chimerical**,*fanciful, imaginary, improbable, foolish*

"What a *chimera* then is man! What a novelty! . . . the glory and the shame of the universe," said Blaise Pascal, a seventeenth-century French mathematician and philosopher. For centuries, philosophers have debated the *chimerical* nature of humankind.

**ECCENTRIC** adj. *decidedly odd or unusual; aberrational* n. *an odd person* pl. **eccentricities**, *oddities, aberrations*

Always try for the part of an *eccentric* in a play, because a quirky character is easier to portray and usually steals the show. Remember the hilarious *eccentricities* of Oscar and Felix in *The Odd Couple*?

**KARMA** n. *your life force that determines your fate or destiny in the next life (Hinduism, Buddhism)*

What is *karma* for the Buddhist is *kismet* for the Arab or Turk. "You must mean predestination," says the Presbyterian. Whether we call it *karma* or something else, everyone would like to explain why life unfolds as it does.

---

**CED/CESS/CEDE = to go, yield**

**precedent**—*any model for that which follows; antecedent*
a legal *precedent*
following a well-known *precedent*

**intercede**—*to come between disputing parties; mediate*
wish someone would *intercede* and end this conflict

Also: **cede, exceed, excess, accede, recede, concede, secede, secession, succeed, process, recess, ancestor, antecedent**

---

**ENIGMA** n. *a riddle hard to puzzle out; conundrum; mystery*
Early in World War II, Churchill broadcast to his English audience: "I cannot forecast to you the action of Russia. It is a riddle wrapped in a mystery inside an *enigma*." And for the modern generation, Russia still appears *enigmatic*.

**VICARIOUS** adj. *felt or experienced secondhand, through someone else or through another medium*
Riding a roller coaster is a real thrill, not a *vicarious* experience. Anyone wanting *vicarious* terror can go to the movies or turn on the TV.

**HYPOTHETICAL** adj. *based on a hypothesis (a logical theory) rather than on reality; conjectural*
Most of our accepted scientific laws began as a logical conjecture, a *hypothetical* "What if . . ." that led to experiments that proved the initial *hypothesis*.

**CRYPTIC** adj. *obscure; intentionally mysterious*
My buddies from Y camp recalled a *cryptic* code we invented one summer. Every summer after that we sent each other *cryptic* messages, especially when we were planning a trip across the lake to the girls' camp.

---

**CHRON = time**

**anachronism**—*a thing out of place in time*
an *anachronism* like the steam engine or a peddler's cart

**chronic**—*habitual, repetitive, long-lasting, frequent*
a *chronic* worrywart
seems to have a *chronic* cold

Also: **chronology, synchronize, chronological, chronicle**

---

**ESOTERIC** adj. *of knowledge belonging to initiated people*
Twins often develop an *esoteric* language that no one else understands.
When I listen to Dad and some of his chemist friends talking, I think that
advanced chemistry has its own *esoteric* vocabulary, too.

**OBLIVIOUS** n. *totally unaware (usu. with "of" or "to")*
Mom accuses us kids of being *oblivious* to dirt and mess. It's not that
we're *oblivious* exactly, it's just that we're more skilled at ignoring that
stuff than most adults.

**UTOPIA** n. *a place where everything about life is perfect*
Meaning "nowhere" in Greek, *utopia* is a place so perfect that it's a pity
it exists only in an old novel. (Dystopia was the place where everything
was as bad as possible.) A great deal of literature centers on *utopian*
longings for an ideal world.

**ELUSIVE** adj. *apt to evade pursuit or definition (as "an elusive
thought"); hard to pin down, identify* v. **elude**
"We seek him here, we seek him there,
Those Frenchies seek him everywhere.
Is he in heaven?—Is he in hell?
That demmed, *elusive* Pimpernel?"
Throughout this swashbuckeling novel by Orczy, the Scarlet Pimpernel
made it his business to *elude* his captors.

## MEMORY FIX
As before, write down each word you don't know, with definitions for
each, and say them all aloud.

## SUBSTITUTION
Replace each italicized word or phrase with the correct word from this
chapter's word and root lists. Change the word's form if necessary for
grammatical correctness.

1.  dispute could last forever unless you *come in between*

    _____

2.  a wounded man, *unaware of* the fight continuing around him

    _____

**3.** gave me a *mysterious* glance I couldn't interpret

_____

**4.** not an actual project yet, purely *based on conjecture*

_____

**5.** a *fantastic* plan that had no prayer of being successful

_____

**6.** lost language of the Druids, along with all their *known only to certain people* lore _____

**7.** don't know whether it was dumb luck or simply my *destiny*

_____

**8.** the *hard to track* fragrance of an elegant perfume

_____

**9.** *extremely odd* behavior that is without *an antecedent*

_____   _____

**10.** a(n) *frequent* yearning for *a perfect place*

_____   _____

## TRUE OR FALSE

Read each sentence to see how the words in this chapter are being used. Then mark **T** (true) or **F** (false) beside each one.

**1.** Shakespeare's reference to a clock on the wall in *Julius Caesar* is an example of an *anachronism* in literature. _____

**2.** Cassandra the *Clairvoyant* would be a good name for the Trojan woman who said, "Beware of Greeks bearing gifts." _____

**3.** The influence of gravity remains a *hypothetical* topic, still under discussion at Dr. Newton's house. _____

4. It hardly requires any *esoteric* information to interpret the Dead Sea scrolls. _____

5. If you're reading a book and fall downstairs, blame it on your bad *karma*, not just inattention. _____

6. Nothing is easier to unravel than a classic *enigma*. _____

7. If I allude to your successful stickup at the bank around my police sergeant uncle, you'd better get ready to *elude* his pursuit. _____

## MATCHING

Circle the two words or phrases that best explain the meaning of each word in bold type.

1. **unprecedented**   illegal   without example   annoying   novel

2. **clairvoyant**   weird   perceptive   a seer   persnickety

3. **eccentric**   unacceptable   fruity   aberrational   odd

4. **cryptic**   undecipherable   enigmatic   deadly   referring to burial

5. **oblivious**   "out to lunch"   clueless   confused   panicky

6. **intercede**   debate   intervene   dispute   mediate

7. **chronic**   repetitive   infectious   long-lasting   tardy

8. **vicarious**   exciting   lively   secondhand   substitutionary

9. **utopian**   ideal   unreal   perfect   impossible

10. **chimerical**   frightening   fanciful   miraculous   imaginary

**Answers for this chapter begin on page 208.**

# LIST 23

# BIG, FAT, GLORIOUS ADJECTIVES

virulent • whimsical • voluminous • ubiquitous • turbulent • haphazard • precocious • vindictive • unimpeachable • voracious • homogeneous • incongruous

**VIRULENT** adj. *full of malignant or evil intent; noted for fast, powerful, often fatal progress*
Tuberculosis, always a *virulent* disease, keeps coming back for another round. Though streptomycin cured the old strains, new and more *virulent* ones require new medication.

**WHIMSICAL** adj. *based on a whim or fancy; capricious*
Sometimes a *whimsical* longing for the ocean comes over me, and a bunch of us pile in the car and head out, even in winter. The occasional *whimsical* idea makes life more fun.

**VOLUMINOUS** adj. *extremely large in volume or size; also, numerous (as in "voluminous notes")*
You don't see *voluminous* skirts anymore, except on some wedding dresses. The only *voluminous* thing in my life right now is the pile of notes for my history paper on the Supreme Court.

**UBIQUITOUS** adj. *seemingly everywhere; widespread*
MacDonald's restaurants, *ubiquitous* today, were scarce just twenty-five years ago. Now the chain has flung its *ubiquitous* Golden Arches over all of Europe, even Russia.

**TURBULENT** adj. *marked by roiling and turmoil and unrest; seething, agitated*
The last half of our senior year is a *turbulent* time when so much is going on. This *turbulence* fills our minds, too, so that finding ways to relax is critical.

---

**ANIMA = mind, soul, spirit**

**animosity**—*hatred, antagonism, ill will, enmity*
    an *animosity* that went back in time
    unjustified *animosity*

**equanimity**—*coolness or evenness of disposition; balance*
    admired the *equanimity* that never deserted him

Also: **animal, animus, animated, unanimous, magnanimous, pusillanimous** *(cowardly)*

---

**HAPHAZARD** adj. *unplanned; happening by chance, at random; aimless* (**hap** = *luck or chance*)
The "hap" words are strewn *haphazardly* throughout the English language. Consider, for example, *happen, happenstance, mayhap, mishap, happy-go-lucky*, and *perhaps*. Originally, *happy* meant "lucky." It's not just a *haphazard* connection, either; of course you'd be happy if you were lucky.

**PRECOCIOUS** adj. *showing very early mental development* (L. = *"precooked" or "prematurely ripe"*)
Everyone hates baby-sitting a kid whose parent brags, "Oh, he's always been *precocious*." The early mastery of language and logic by the *precocious* child is a lousy excuse for rude behavior.

---

**VI/VIT/VIV = life**

**viable**—*capable of living; able to work or develop acceptably or even well*
        a *viable* fetus
        a *viable* product
        a *viable* candidate

**convivial**—*friendly and lively of spirit, party-loving*
        a noisy, *convivial* gathering
        her open, *convivial* nature

Also: **vital, vitamin, revitalize, vitality, vivid, revive, vivisection, vivacity, vivacious**

---

**VINDICTIVE** adj. *eager for revenge; spiteful*
A *vindictive* spirit keeps a fight going, such as the famous Hatfield-McCoy feud in Appalachia. And isn't there something awfully *vindictive* about the ancient code of Hammurabi, which read, "An eye for an eye; a tooth for a tooth"?

**UNIMPEACHABLE** adj. *blameless, irreproachable; not open to accusation*
For my history paper, I went to an *unimpeachable* source of Supreme Court information: a sitting Justice. If a Justice's honor isn't absolutely *unimpeachable*, then no one's is.

**VORACIOUS** adj. *insatiably hungry for something; ravenous*
Kids who "tear up" the SATs and PSATs are the ones who've always been *voracious* readers. Greg's been a *voracious* eater for the last six years; now he's working on the reading.

**HOMOGENEOUS** adj. *being the same or alike throughout (lit. "the same kind"); also,* homogenous
Countries such as Sweden and Denmark tend to be extremely *homogeneous*, while the United States is less *homogenized* every day as the unhappy from afar find refuge here. Diversity of people makes life more interesting, but it is also more challenging than *homogeneity*.

**INCONGRUOUS** adj. *seeming out of place or unsuited*
A tuxedo would look totally *incongruous* in our school, except on Live Character Day. That day, we all dressed as our favorite literary character, and nothing seemed *incongruous*, especially not the terrific pig costume I wore as Wilbur.

## MEMORY FIX
You know the routine. Write down each word you don't know, along with its definition, and say each word aloud.

## FILL-IN CHART

Fill in the missing boxes with information learned in this chapter.

| Word | Prefix/Root | Two Synonyms/ Definition |
|---|---|---|
| 1. | **dic/dict** = say | revengeful, |
| 2. turbulent | **turb** = agitate | |
| 3. | **homo** = same **gen** = kind | same or alike throughout |
| 4. | **anim** = spirit, soul | enmity, |
| 5. | **hap** = luck, chance | |
| 6. | **equ** = equal, same **anim** = spirit, soul | |
| 7. virulent | **virus** = poison | |
| 8. convivial | **con** = with; **viv** = life | |
| 9. | **ubique** = everywhere | everywhere, |
| 10. precocious | **pre** = before **coquere** = cooked | |

## RHYME TIME

Complete these lines of admittedly awful poetry with words from this chapter's list.

1. In the narrow coal shaft, hunting bituminous
   Forswear all garments considered _____.

2. Vicki suffered for hours from insects _____,
   She dug at the bites and swore, Goodness Gracious!
   Smearing her body with calamine lotion
   Was more than just a _____ notion.

3. It's an overused buzzword; I refuse to be liable,
   That tired, _____ adjective

   _____.

4. Our purebred came with papers _____,
   Sad to say, he has proved unteachable.

5. Students teaching classes is not an _____
   thought,
   We remember well what our peers have taught.

## WORD ANALYSIS

Fill in the most logical word for each sentence, choosing from among the words presented in this chapter.

1. The child who is reading at age three is usually described as

   _____.

2. In the middle of a memorial service, giddy laughter would seem
   not only _____, but also irreverent.

3. Thomas á Becket, who did not accede to all of Henry II's wishes,
   was murdered in Canterbury Cathedral not long after Henry
   allegedly cried, "Who will rid me of the t_____
   priest?"

4. Elementary kids have a _____ appetite for
   information about dinosaurs.

5. You can tell that comedian Robin Williams gives in to
   _____ flights of fancy as they occur to him, ad
   libbing with a brilliance given only to a few.

6. Universally, people revere magnanimity and fear those with a
   _____ streak.

**Answers for this chapter begin on page 209.**

# GOULASH

---

**paradigm • unscathed • iconoclast • kindle • elaborate • tacit • peripheral • deter • propensity • discord • precipitate • unethical**

---

**PARADIGM** n. *something serving as a model or ideal*
For years, our class unknowingly acted as a *paradigm* for classes after us. We didn't plan to be a model class, but we gradually realized that we were the acknowledged *paradigm*.

**UNSCATHED** adj. *unharmed, uninjured, untouched* adj. **scathing**, *bitterly severe, caustic*
No class is perfect, and ours won't graduate *unscathed*. This spring, our most outspoken students delivered some *scathing* criticism of the school to local newspaper reporters.

**ICONOCLAST** n. *one who criticizes established ideas or traditions (Gr. = image destroyer)*
These talkative students were known *iconoclasts*, of course, who'd rebelled for various reasons all through school. But we understood their *iconoclastic* views from long association and had always respected their ideas.

**KINDLE** v. *to start burning; to spark interest or curiosity*
Nothing *kindles* the interest of the public like a hot newspaper story. Our classmates' best suggestions for school reform *kindled* a desire in several parents to begin discussions with the school administration.

**ELABORATE** v. *to spell out specifically, in detail* adj. *detailed or complex; carefully planned*
Those interested parents asked our reform-minded classmates to *elaborate* on their ideas. While some of their concepts were too *elaborate* to implement, many of their suggestions met with approval, even requests for further *elaboration*.

---

### SED/SESS/SID = to sit or be still

**assiduous**—*marked by careful, diligent attention; persistent*
  *assiduously* cleaning his fur
  giving it *assiduous* attention

**insidious**—*dangerous but appealing; slow but steady in effect; subtle; settling in unnoticed (as in "an insidious disease")*
  an *insidious* illness
  the *insidious* lure of gambling

Also: **sedentary, sediment, supersede, preside, subsidy, dissident, resident, session, obsession, sedate**

---

**TACIT** adj. *understood though not spoken; silent*
Students and parents arrived at a *tacit* agreement that the parents would advance these novel ideas. Everyone *tacitly* acknowledged that parents would receive more serious attention from school officials.

**PERIPHERAL** adj. *around the edge or periphery; auxiliary; of minor, not central, importance*
The parents' committee decided to deal with only a few central issues and to ignore the *peripheral* ones. Just as *peripheral* (side) vision is less critical than forward vision, some of the students' ideas were less important.

**DETER** v. *to hinder or prevent from acting; to inhibit, turn aside or discourage* n. **deterrent**
Nothing would *deter* my parents from joining this group of adults bent on change. I had hoped that my begging for noninvolvement would be a *deterrent*, but it wasn't.

---

### TEND/TENS/TENT = to stretch

**tenuous**—*slight and insubstantial; flimsy, weak*
  only a *tenuous* grasp of the subject
  new and *tenuous* idea

**extenuating**—*mitigating; reducing in severity or importance*
  an *extenuating* circumstance that explained her lateness

Also: **tendency, extend, extension, portent, portentous, contend, contentious, tension, tense, pretense**

---

**PROPENSITY** n. *strong natural leaning or preference*
Have you noticed how your parents have a *propensity* for getting involved when you wish they wouldn't? The natural *propensity* of ostriches is to stick their heads in the sand, hoping to go unnoticed, but parents sure aren't like that.

**DISCORD** n. *lack of agreement or harmony; strife, tension*
The night the parents met with the school officials was marked at first by *discord*. The seeds of this *discord* had been sown by the newspaper story, of course.

**PRECIPITATE** v. *to cause to begin in an abrupt manner* adj. *unwisely fast, impetuous, headlong*
Although the newspaper article *precipitated* the parents' involvement with school policy, no one at the meeting wanted to plunge *precipitately* into massive changes.

**UNETHICAL** adj. *lacking moral principles (ethics)*
Closed meetings of public boards are *unethical* in our state. The "Sunshine Laws" insist that the operations—and therefore the *ethics*—of ruling boards should be open to scrutiny by their employers, the taxpayers.

## MEMORY FIX
Now's the time to write down each word in this chapter that you don't know, along with its definition. Say each word aloud too. Remember why you're doing this? WRITING FIXES WORDS IN MIND.

## FILL IN THE BLANKS
From the new words in this chapter, select the one that best completes the meaning and logic of each phrase. Be sure to use the right form of each word.

1. there'll be a reason, some _____ explanation

2. always questioned authority, a(n) _____ from birth

3. suspected of _____ behavior in office

4. hoping to _____ a creative fire to last all autumn

5. a real enigma that needs precise _____ (use the noun)

6. didn't actually say yes, but nodded in _____ approval

7. a(n) _____ weed that seemed to spread overnight

8. so weak now that she has but a(n) _____ hold on life

9. cannot do drugs and expect to escape _____

10. a cat's inherited _____ for hunting prey

## MATCHING ANTONYMS

From the word list below, find an opposite for each numbered word and write it on the appropriate line.

traditionalist    kindle      deter      discord   elaborate
precipitate    peripheral    careless    spoken    honorable

1. unethical _____

2. central, main _____

3. douse _____

4. simple _____

5. harmony _____

6. encourage _____

7. tacit _____

8. considered _____

9. assiduous _____

10. iconoclast _____

## MATCHING

In the group of words at the right, find two synonyms or phrases to write beside each of the words to the left.

**1.** scathing     _____      dangerously alluring

                 _____      flimsy

                                             lack of harmony

**2.** propensity     _____      impetuous

                 _____      discourage

                                               model

**3.** peripheral     _____      caustic

                 _____      strife

                                               admired example

**4.** discord     _____      tendency

                 _____      persistent

                                               headlong

**5.** tenuous     _____      most attentive

                 _____      inhibit

                                               barely perceptible

**6.** deter     _____      auxiliary

                 _____      highly critical

                                               subtle

**7.** insidious     _____      around the edge

                 _____      inclination

**8.** paradigm     _____

                 _____

**9.** precipitate     _____

                 _____

**10.** assiduous     _____

                 _____

**Answers for this chapter begin on page 209.**

---

arbitrary • blatant • capricious • desultory •
extraneous • flagrant • devious • compatible •
detrimental • susceptible • resigned • sporadic

---

**ARBITRARY** adj. *according to choice or impulse, rather than merit; in a tyrannical or despotic way*
I made an *arbitrary* decision to serve pizza at the class party. When there isn't a chance to consult a group or take a vote, I prefer to make an *arbitrary* choice and not worry about it.

**BLATANT** adj. *embarrassingly obvious, loud, or showy; brazen, tasteless*
Nobody likes to make a *blatant* error in public because it's embarrassing. Showing up in clothes that prove to be *blatantly* out of place, for instance, is pretty awkward.

**CAPRICIOUS** adj. *not steady, changing on a whim or "caprice"*
The stereotype of a female movie star is that of a *capricious* airhead. Actually, a good actress tries to be wholly professional and leaves *capricious* behavior to butterflies.

**DESULTORY** adj. *in a random, unplanned fashion; haphazard*
Last weekend we struck off into the woods on a long, *desultory* ramble that took us to a creek we'd never seen before. That's the fun of excursions done in a *desultory* way; you never know what you'll discover.

**EXTRANEOUS** adj. *extra, nonessential, irrelevant*
"No *extraneous* chitchat," said the guidance counselor as he blue-penciled my essay for a college application. "Make a careful outline, then don't add even one *extraneous* word!"

---

**HER/HES = to cling, stick**

coherent—*logically arranged or ordered; lucid (clear)*
   now *coherent* after the accident
   a helpful, *coherent* talk

inherent—*natural, inborn, innate*
   an *inherent* ability to swim
   an *inherently* cheerful soul

Also: **adhere, adhesive, cohesive, incoherent, adherent**

---

**FLAGRANT** adj. *highly noticeable in a negative way; glaring*
Occasionally, Meatloaf goes for a stroll on the kitchen counters in *flagrant* disobedience of house rules. Cats are known for following their own interests, of course, no matter how *flagrant* their behavior.

**DEVIOUS** adj. *indirect, roundabout; cunning or deceptive; remote (as "a devious path through the woods")*
I can follow a trail, no matter how *devious*, but not the twists and turns of a *devious* mind. Perhaps the most infamous *devious* thinker was Nicolo Machiavelli; anything termed Machiavellian is noted for its cunning or duplicity.

**COMPATIBLE** adj. *well-suited; adaptable; related, similar*
Dogs and cats are supposed to be *incompatible*, but families with pets know better. A cat and dog raised together may be not only *compatible* but also very attached to one another. (Remember *The Incredible Journey*?)

---

**CID/CIS = to cut; to kill**

concise—*short and to the point; succinct; admirably brief*
   a *concise*, effective speech
   with delightful *conciseness*

incisive—*decisive, direct, and forceful in approach*
   an *incisive* analysis
   an *incisive* decision-maker

Also: **decide, decisive, incise, incision, excise, excision, precise, precision, homicide, fratricide, matricide**

---

**DETRIMENTAL** adj. *definitely harmful; damaging; pernicious*
Spraying hedgerows and ditches to kill weeds proved sadly *detrimental* to game birds like pheasants who lost their nesting sites. Modern ecologists know that we must stop any practice that is a *detriment* to our nation's wildlife.

**SUSCEPTIBLE** adj. *open to, subject to, or responsive to; impressionable; liable*
I tan easily, so I didn't believe I was *susceptible* to a bad sunburn. Wrong again, Ted. That same camp-out taught me that I had an extreme *susceptibility* to poison ivy, too.

**RESIGNATION** n. *acceptance of the inevitable or the obvious; submissiveness, surrender; formal notice of leaving a job or a responsibility*
Mom is finally *resigned* to the idea that I'll be working out of town this summer. "Your last summer at home," she said, with a sigh of weary *resignation*. "Parents *resign* themselves to the fact that kids grow and go—but it happens so fast."

**SPORADIC** adj. *occurring off and on; inconstant*
Dad said, "Ted'll be home *sporadically* over the summer." "You can count on me, Ma," I assured her. "It won't be *sporadic* either. I need to do laundry and eat real food at least every other weekend."

## MEMORY FIX
Need we say it? Write them, stare at them, write their meanings, say them aloud.

## SUBSTITUTION
Replace each italicized word or phrase with the correct word from this chapter.

1. You should consult all the club members, not just make a(n) *tryrannical* decision. _____

2. I was leafing through the anthology in a *random, unplanned* way when I found an incredible poem. _____

3. Spilling that after-shave lotion on my dresser was *extremely harmful* to the oak finish. _____

4. My mind must have wandered during the math test, because I made a *badly noticeable* error on an easy problem.

_____

5. We may be *forced to face the inevitable* to our principal's leaving, but we don't have to like it. _____

6. I made some *off and on* attempts to pick up my room, but I got distracted and never finished. _____

7. The bee doesn't really flit in a(n) *unsteady, whimsical* way from flower to flower; she just looks disorganized.

_____

8. Reggie's always advertising his store in such a *loud, embarrassingly pushy* way that I would never shop there.

_____

9. It's tough to accept the idea of our *innately* imperfect nature until you watch toddlers push each other around.

_____

10. Somebody should teach our manager how to deliver a(n) *decisively cutting to the heart of the matter* speech.

_____

## TRUE OR FALSE

Read each sentence to see how the words in this chapter are being used. Then mark **T** (true) or **F** (false) beside each.

1. If you wore a little asafetida bag the way kids did in "the old days," you wouldn't be *susceptible* to colds. _____

2. Teachers enjoy students who *flagrantly* flout school rules.

_____

3. The Pony Express would have been more efficient if it had operated in a more *desultory* or *capricious* manner. _____

4. A landscaper with an inherently *devious* mind could prove to be a natural designer of garden mazes. _____

5. My painfully shy, withdrawn Aunt Willy would have communicated better with a more *incisive* psychologist. _____

6. Snakes and mice are naturally *compatible*. _____

## MATCHING

Circle the two words or phrases that best explain the meaning of each word in bold type.

1. **coherent**   sticky   logical   buddy   lucid   inaudible

2. **concise**   succinct   clear   cohesive   brief   meager

3. **devious**   putrid   criminal   roundabout   unattractive   crafty

4. **compatible**   agreeable   comfortable   positive   well-suited   convivial

5. **susceptible**   underdone   ailing   confused by   liable   receptive to

6. **extraneous**   irrelevant   nonessential   critical   central   abundant

7. **inherent**   hairless   hirsute   inborn   basic   natural

8. **blatant**   delayed   "loud"   hereditary   glaring   stupid

9. **sporadic**   moldy   druggie   topmost story   irregular   inconstant

10. **arbitrary**   despotic   mediating   impulsive   convenient   selective

**Answers for this chapter begin on page 209.**

# LISTS 21-25 REVIEW

The preceding five lists featured words you'll use for the rest of your life . . . and maybe on the SAT in a few weeks. Read each of those lists again to refresh your memory before completing this oh-so-helpful review.

## ANALOGIES

Circle the one word pair in each list below that expresses the same relationship as the pair in capital letters.

1. **TIME : ANACHRONISTIC**
   - (A) era : mesozoic
   - (B) place : ubiquitous
   - (C) theory : hypothetical
   - (D) setting : incongruous
   - (E) country : utopian

2. **PROPHET : CLAIRVOYANT**
   - (A) tyrant : frugal
   - (B) paradigm : exemplary
   - (C) instructor : incisive
   - (D) architect : ethical
   - (E) iconoclast : vindictive

3. **APPARENT : FLAGRANT**
   - (A) brief : concise
   - (B) ubiquitous : omnipresent
   - (C) detrimental : harmful
   - (D) careful : assiduous
   - (E) sporadic : desultory

4. **WATER : TURBULENT**
   - (A) knowledge : esoteric
   - (B) excuse : extenuating
   - (C) decision : imprudent
   - (D) reason : unethical
   - (E) thought : incoherent

5. **APPETITE : VORACIOUS**
   - (A) milk : homogeneous
   - (B) apparel : voluminous
   - (C) mind : oblivious
   - (D) route : devious
   - (E) talent : minimal

6. **EXTRANEOUS : DETAIL**
   - (A) peripheral : issue
   - (B) animated : cartoon
   - (C) elusive : enigma
   - (D) generic : drug
   - (E) ingenuous : idea

# FIND THE ODDBALL

In each word group, cross out the oddball, the one unrelated word or phrase.

1. genetic   gentleman   ingenious   brilliant   congenial

2. destiny   kismet   karma   predestination   fate   prophecy

3. conjectural   theoretical   hypothetical   pragmatic

4. fleeting   elusive   evasive   running   slippery

5. intending evil   malignant   swiftly powerful   virulent   hideous

6. unscathed   not touched   fragile   uninjured   harmful

7. spark   ignite   energize   elucidate   kindle   excite

8. alternate   discourage   inhibit   hinder   deter

9. erroneous   rash   impetuous   precipitate   headlong

10. indigent   brazen   tasteless   loud   blatant   showy

11. crooked   cunning   twisted   indirect   devious   inspired

12. forceful   direct   decisive   incisive   reclusive

# WHO SAID THAT?

From the choices offered, select the type of speaker for each of the following comments.

pragmatist      credulous one   clairvoyant   pious one
eccentric       arbitrary one   iconoclast    vindictive one
convivial soul

1. There, but for the grace of God, go I. _____

2. Oil paints are a silly tradition; I paint with mud. _____

3. You will go on a long journey. _____

4. How about a little dessert before dinner? _____

5. Why? Because I said so! (All parents are eventually driven to this, you know.) _____

6. Very sensible approach. I like it. _____

7. The ad promised I'd lose ten pounds in five days.

_____

8. I'll get you for that. _____

9. Yo, Goombah, let's party! _____

## FIND THE SYNONYMS

From the word list below, choose two more synonyms to complete each group.

| | | | | |
|---|---|---|---|---|
| chimerical | frugal | propensity | desultory | tenuous |
| enigmatic | congenial | fanciful | parochial | cryptic |
| whimsical | thrifty | tendency | capricious | narrow |
| tacit | flimsy | compatible | haphazard | unspoken |

1. like-minded _____ sociable _____

2. inconstant _____ fanciful _____

3. random _____ unplanned _____

4. obscure _____ mysterious _____

5. sparing _____ prudent _____

6. provincial _____ limited _____

**7.** insubstantial _____    slight _____

**8.** silent _____    understood _____

**9.** natural leaning _____    inclination _____

**10.** imaginary _____    improbable _____

## THE ROOT OF IT ALL

Here's the root, with a blank for every missing letter and a definition for a clue.

| | |
|---|---|
| **1.** _ _ **hes** _ _ _ | gluey or sticky |
| **2. gen** _ _ _ | brilliant person |
| **3.** _ _ **gen** _ _ _ _ | innocent, naive, gullible |
| **4. gen** _ | transmitter of hereditary factors |
| **5.** _ _ **gen** _ _ _ | to foster, begin |
| **6. gen** _ _ _ _ | of a general type or class |
| **7.** _ _ _ _ _ **gen** _ _ _ _ | faking honesty |
| **8. cred** _ _ _ _ | worthy of being believed |
| **9.** _ _ _ _ _ **ced** _ | to mediate between disputants |
| **10. chron** _ _ | habitual, long-lasting |
| **11. anim** _ _ _ _ _ | bitter antagonism |
| **12.** _ _ _ **anim** _ _ _ | of a balanced, even disposition |
| **13.** _ _ **sid** _ _ _ _ | dangerously alluring; subtle |
| **14.** _ _ **ten** _ _ _ _ _ _ | reducing in severity or importance |
| **15.** _ _ **cis** _ _ _ | cutting teeth |

**Answers for this review lesson begin on page 210.**

# LIST 26

# BOLSTER, DON'T CARP

exhaust • enervate • carp • coerce • bolster • belittle • advocate • cajole • facilitate • denounce • deplete • alienate

**EXHAUST** v. *to use up entirely; deplete; to wear out physically*
adj. **exhaustive,** *thorough*
Nothing is more *exhausting* than college applications. My brain *exhausted* all of its ideas for essays on the first few schools. Also, each form requires such an *exhaustive* roundup of information that it would *exhaust* anyone's patience.

**ENERVATE** v. *to drain of energy and mental quickness*
Totally *enervated* after spending hours on these applications, I sacked out for a little power nap. Filling in miles of forms had been *enervating* beyond belief.

**CARP** v. *to nag in a petty, nitpicky way; to find fault*
I woke up to hear Mom *carping* about the applications being due right now. "Hey, Ma," I said when I could get a word in, "don't *carp* at me. I'm working, I'm working!"

**COERCE** v. *to force or compel (someone or something)*
"We can't *coerce* you into hurrying," Mom said, "but it's so much smarter to turn the applications in early. Sorry about the nagging. *Coercion* isn't our style here, you know."

**BOLSTER** v. *to act as a support or prop; to reinforce*
I was feeling pretty sorry for myself, so I said, "Yeah, I need major *bolstering* right now, not criticism. Being a senior is tough; we all need to be *bolstered* now and then."

**BELITTLE** v. *to make fun of or reduce in importance; to disparage or decry*
"Oh, boo hoo," Mom said, grinning. "I hate to *belittle* your problems, but you could be worse off—such as not graduating and not going to college. Still, you'll never find me *belittling* the work those applications take."

---

**CAP/CIP/CEPT = to take, get**

**incipient**—*beginning to be; commencing*
    an *incipient* cold
    the *incipient* signs of spring

**perceptive**—*keenly observant; discerning; very understanding*
    my most *perceptive* friend
    a *perceptive* analysis

Also: **capture, captivate, caption, anticipate, reciprocate, emancipate, intercept, receptive, susceptible**

---

**ADVOCATE** v. *to support, recommend, be in favor of* n. *a person who pleads a case; lawyer*
Coming from Mom, who's always been my staunchest *advocate*, that was okay, but not terrific. However, she *advocates* total honesty within the family, and that's what I got.

**CAJOLE** v. *to beg earnestly, to wheedle or coax*
Hoping to *cajole* her into helping, I said, "I could really use just a teensy bit of—" and watched her shake her head. "No amount of *cajolery* will work this time. If you can't do the applications, you aren't ready for those schools."

**FACILITATE** v. *to make easier or simpler, to smooth the way*
"To *facilitate* your process," Mom suggested, "try using the school memories book that we've always kept. You'll get ideas from way back in kindergarten, and I'm sure that will *facilitate* the writing of all those essays."

---

**FER = to carry, bear, bring**

**infer**—*to conclude from available evidence; to deduce, guess*
    *infer* his meaning from his tone
    can *infer* when he's tired

**proliferate**—*to multiply, increase rapidly in number*
    cancerous cells that *proliferate*
    a *proliferation* of schools

Also: **confer, conference, vociferous, transfer, coniferous (cone-bearing), proffer, offer, defer, deference**

---

**DENOUNCE** v. *to criticize, especially publicly; to accuse* n. **denunciation**, *negative criticism*

The record book was a great help, but inwardly I found myself *denouncing* college applications on all counts. It was a truly exhaustive *denunciation*; I didn't leave out any of the parts that I thought were most annoying.

**DEPLETE** v. *to greatly reduce any supply; to drain, bankrupt, or impoverish* n. **depletion**

By the time I finished all seven sets of forms, I had *depleted* my store of memories, my list of accomplishments, and my supply of good humor. My enthusiasm for going away to college had suffered some *depletion*, too, but it soon returned to bolster my spirits.

**ALIENATE** v. *to estrange, set apart by ill will (affections or people who had once been close)*

On discovering that I was one of the few who had finished all of his college applications, I kept quiet for fear of *alienating* my friends. Usually, I'd rather not mention something than *alienate* people.

## MEMORY FIX
Once again, write each word you don't know, with a definition for each, then say the words aloud.

## FILL IN THE BLANKS
From the new words in this chapter, select the one that best completes the meaning and logic of each sentence. Change the form of the word as required for correctness.

1. A long hike is _____ for the trained hiker only if some emergency forces him to _____ his energy early in the hike.

2. I don't mean to _____ your work, but picking up your room will probably not make the *Guinness Book of Records*.

3. Our family's tired of the constantly _____ critics on TV and in newspapers, who apparently never approve of anyone or anything.

4. We stayed with Amy until she went into surgery, hoping to
_____ her spirits about losing her wisdom teeth.

5. "I can _____ from the look of your faces," she said,
"that I'm not going to feel so hot when the anesthetic wears off."

6. Ever since she was little, Amy's been unusually
_____ when it comes to reading faces.

7. General anesthesia drains me of energy for days afterward, so for
me it has a seriously _____ effect.

8. In the dental recovery room, I could detect small bulges in Amy's
cheeks, _____ signs of the swelling to come.

9. Hoping to _____ recovery by reducing swelling
and pain, we held ice packs to Amy's cheeks.

10. No amount of _____ would have made Amy eat
those first hours after surgery, but eventually we
_____ her into drinking a milkshake.

## ANTONYMS

You'll recognize some of these antonyms from past lists as you make the
match of opposites.

| | | |
|---|---|---|
| _____ | 1. bolster | acclaim |
| _____ | 2. deplete | energize |
| _____ | 3. denounce | dull, obtuse |
| _____ | 4. incipient | contain |
| _____ | 5. facilitate | undermine |
| _____ | 6. perceptive | extol |
| _____ | 7. enervate | terminal, final |
| _____ | 8. proliferate | hamper, hinder |
| _____ | 9. carp | replenish |

# SWITCHEROO

Many words in this lesson, in addition to being verbs, are also nouns and adjectives. Match these equally important words with their meanings.

| | | |
|---|---|---|
| _____ | 1. alienation | supporter |
| _____ | 2. advocacy | keenness |
| _____ | 3. depletion | conclusion, deduction |
| _____ | 4. perceptiveness | estrangement |
| _____ | 5. advocate | wheedling, begging |
| _____ | 6. proliferation | force |
| _____ | 7. inference | sponsorship, support |
| _____ | 8. denunciation | exhaustion |
| _____ | 9. cajolery | (rapid) multiplication |
| _____ | 10. coercion | negative criticism |

**Answers for this chapter begin on page 211.**
Answers for this chapter begin on page 211.

---

bizarre • prosaic • zany • static • urbane • opaque •
stoic • subtle • latent • innate • futile • candid

---

**BIZARRE** adj. *strikingly unusual or incongruous; fantastic or jolting in impact*
Our word *bizarre* was once *bizarro*, Spanish for "brave" or "handsome," and also *bizar* for the Basques, who greatly admired beards. Not the French; they loathed beards and termed the Basques *bizarre*, meaning "strange."

**PROSAIC** adj. *ordinary, unexciting, dull, unimaginative*
I've led an awfully predictable, *prosaic* life so far. I'd like to do a year of college studies abroad, which would be foreign and exciting, not at all *prosaic*.

**ZANY** adj. *wacky, absurd, ludicrous, "crazy"*
*Zany*, a nickname for Giovanni (John), was a common way to address servants in sixteenth-century Italy. In their local plays, a clowning servant was a *Zani*, who always made a fool of his master. What a *zany* history for a word!

**STATIC** adj. *unchanging; quiet, at rest; stationary, fixed;* n. *electronic noise; back talk (slang)*
The last chem experiment concerned solutions that remained *static* in spite of various attempts to destabilize them. When you think about it, not much in life remains *static*.

**URBANE** adj. *smooth and sophisticated (said of men); suave*
From the Latin *urbs* (city) comes *urbane* to describe a polished city fellow, the opposite of a country hick. Once, actor David Niven was considered the epitome of the *urbane* male. (See the tape of *Around the World in 80 Days*.)

---

**ANTHROP = man, human being**

**misanthrope**—*one who hates people or distrusts them*
the attitudes of a confirmed *misanthrope*

**philanthropy**—*generous donation of time or money to benefit others (lit. love for human beings)*
the famous *philanthropist* Andrew Carnegie

Also: **anthropoid, anthropology, anthropomorphism**

---

**OPAQUE** adj. *difficult to explain or to understand; mentally slow, obtuse, thick-skulled; also, not allowing light to pass through* n. **opacity**
The beautiful characters that make up the Chinese and the Japanese languages often appear daunting, even *opaque* to Westerners like me. I hate to think that I'm the one who's *opaque*, so I'll probably try to learn Japanese in college.

**STOIC** adj. *showing no feeling or pain; impassive*
Taking their name from the porch (*stoa*) where they met, the old Greek *Stoics* were taught by Zeno to be indifferent to passion or pain and to accept calmly whatever happened in life. People who could *stoically* ignore pain probably fared much better in ancient times.

---

**AC/ACR = sharp**

**acute**—*sharp or pointed; keenly perceptive (as "an acute eye")*
an *acute* commentary
family known for their *acute* minds

**acrimonious**—*bitterly sharp, rancorous, biting*
an unusually *acrimonious* remark
based on *acrimony*

**exacerbate**—*to make (a condition) worse; to aggravate*
don't *exacerbate* that sprain
illness *exacerbated* by worry

Also: **acrid, acrimony, acerbic, acumen** (All SAT favorites!)

---

**SUBTLE** adj. *not obvious in any way; elusive; hard to under-stand (as "a subtle language"); keenly discerning (as "subtle interpretation"); extremely clever; behaving in an insidious way (as "a subtle disease")*
Both cancer and AIDS are diseases feared for their *subtlety*. Scores of the country's *subtlest* medical minds are concentrated on these dreaded ailments.

**LATENT** adj. *hidden, submerged, waiting to be aroused or discovered; inactive, dormant, potential*
Throughout school, I kept hoping that good coaching would uncover a *latent* talent for some sport, preferably wrestling. But whatever I've got in the way of *latent* ability is still dormant, so now I'm looking for a sport that's just fun.

**INNATE** adj. *inborn, inherent, natural*
An *innately* talented composer, Mozart wrote music with skill and confidence before age 5. In the remaining thirty years of his life, he created over 600 compositions, many of which have an *innate* perfection of form that remains unmatched.

**FUTILE** adj. *ineffective, useless; vain (as "a futile hope")* n. **futility** (*Note:* utile = useful)
I've wasted a lot of time in *futile* tasks, such as trying to keep my room neat. I'm going to abandon this exercise in *futility*, because the room feels weird when it's too tidy.

**CANDID** adj. *honest, open, without guile or deceit; frank, even blunt* n. **candor**
Poet George Canning wrote, "Save, save, oh save me from the *candid* friend!" as a reminder that it's possible to be too frank with someone close to you. Sometimes a friend needs more thoughtfulness and a lot less *candor*.

## MEMORY FIX
Here we go again. Write down each word you don't know; write its meaning, and say each one aloud.

## TRUE OR FALSE
Read each sentence below to see how the new words in this chapter are being used. Then mark **T** (true) or **F** (false) beside each one.

**1.** The best tone for a thank-you note is one of *acrimony*. _____

2. More rain will only *exacerbate* our current drought. _____

3. You'd better hope your dentist is not a *misanthrope*. _____

4. No one ever exhibits a trained rabbit, leading us to infer that bunnies are not overly *acute*. _____

5. "Mind over matter" is an apt motto for the *stoic*. _____

6. Many allegedly *futile* projects, such as going to the moon, have been accomplished; more will probably follow. _____

7. The opposite of misanthropy is *philanthropy*. _____

8. The caveman's stout club was proof of his innate *subtlety*. _____

9. Prepare to put on a *stoic* face if someone begins a conversation like this: "In all *candor* I feel I must tell you that. . . ." _____ _____

10. Chances are, everyone has *latent* abilities. _____

## FIND THE SYNONYMS

From the word list below, add the correct synonyms to each numbered group by writing them on the appropriate lines.

| | | | | |
|---|---|---|---|---|
| dull-witted | inborn | guileless | suave | ordinary |
| unimaginative | insidious | shocking | potential | ludicrous |
| very clever | dormant | absurd | inherent | fantastic |
| sophisticated | obtuse | unchanging | frank | stationary |

1. bizarre   incongruous   odd

_____    _____

2. prosaic   dull   humdrum

_____    _____

**3.** zany   wacko   crazy

_____   _____

**4.** static   fixed   quiet

_____   _____

**5.** urbane   polished   smooth

_____   _____

**6.** opaque   hard to penetrate or understand

_____   _____

**7.** subtle   elusive   very discerning

_____   _____

**8.** latent   hidden   inactive

_____   _____

**9.** innate   natural

_____   _____

**10.** candid   open   honest

_____   _____

## SUBSTITUTION

For the words or phrases in italics, substitute the correct words from this chapter's word list.

1. There's nothing _dull or commonplace_ about that checkout girl; it's an orangutan in a(n) _outlandish_ costume.

   _____   _____

2. He may be a(n) _polished_, well-dressed fellow, but under that designer haircut is an exceedingly _dim-witted_ brain.

   _____   _____

3. The *frank, open* comments of that hockey player with the *impervious to pain* look on his face led to a(n) *bitterly cutting* exchange. _____  _____

_____

4. Don't give me any *negative noise* on that decision.

_____

5. We've suggested that our *wacko* Aunt Jolly change her ways, but it's *useless* to even talk to her.

_____  _____

**Answers for this chapter begin on page 211.**

quizzical • rigorous • reprehensible • salutary • prolific • recalcitrant • pedestrian • unassailable • volatile • superfluous • obsolete • diffident

**QUIZZICAL** adj. *teasing, but questioning too; puzzled*
"You're in charge of Senior Weekend?" Mom said with a *quizzical* look. "Tell me you're kidding!" Of course, I wasn't teasing, and her look went from *quizzical* to concerned.

**RIGOROUS** adj. *demanding or strict in requirements; absolutely accurate and precise; harsh (climate)*
"We'll expect you to keep *rigorous* accounts of all your expenses," the senior adviser told me. Any way I looked at it, I had taken on an extremely *rigorous* task.

**REPREHENSIBLE** adj. *deserving blame or criticism*
Then I had a *reprehensible* thought: What if I said I couldn't plan Senior Weekend after all? What was really *reprehensible* of me—and just plain dumb—was thinking that I could do this job without a committee of helpers.

**SALUTARY** adj. *promoting good health (mental or physical)*
The idea of helpers was so *salutary* that I cheered up and went in search of a committee. The five of us met over burgers and fries—tasty, though not very *salutary*—to discuss ideas for the weekend after graduation.

**PROLIFIC** adj. *very productive or fruitful; fertile, fecund*
*Prolific* critters such as mice and rabbits produce an impressive number of progeny. So do *prolific* minds create ideas; my committee suggested so many that we had trouble deciding what to do.

---

**FLU/FLUX/FLUCT = to flow**

**mellifluous**—*sweetly or smoothly flowing (of sounds or voices)*
    a *mellifluous* vocalist
    instrument with *mellifluous* tones

**fluent**—*gifted in speaking; graceful in movement; polished*
    a *fluent* speaker of French
    the *fluent* body of a gymnast

Also: **affluent, fluid, fluctuate, influence, confluence, effluent, effluvium, influx, flux, fluxion**

---

**RECALCITRANT** adj. *very tough to control; defiant of authority; unruly, refractory*
Four of us agreed on a great idea, but one *recalcitrant* kid said no. As I wondered how to win him over, I remembered that he'd been pretty stubborn and *recalcitrant* ever since kindergarten.

**PEDESTRIAN** adj. *commonplace, ordinary, unimaginative; referring to going by foot (as "a pedestrian walk")*
"Renting an old, broken-down camp for the weekend," Harold grumbled. "That's so ho-hum . . . so *pedestrian*! For once, can't we do something that isn't so boringly *pedestrian*?"

**UNASSAILABLE** adj. *not assailable; not open to attack, to question, or to doubt*
Jodie grinned. "Pedestrian, huh? Well, troops, we now have *unassailable* proof that Harold prepped for SATs." "Very funny," he retorted. "Also *unassailable* is the fact that we still haven't got a good idea!"

---

**SPIC/SPEC/SPECT = to look, see**

**conspicuous**—*very noticeable; commanding attention, striking*
    *conspicuous* by his absence
    a *conspicuous* display of talent

**circumspect**—*cautious, watchful, careful, and prudent*
    take the time needed for a *circumspect* decision

Also: **auspicious, suspicion, perspicacity, perspicuous, spectator, inspection, speculation, specious**

**VOLATILE** adj. *quick to express emotion; explosive, easily triggered (a chemical or a person's temper); changeable, unstable*

Now here's a *volatile* guy for you, I thought, wondering why I hadn't remembered Harold's quick temper. The other aspect of his *volatility*, however, was changeability, and as Jodie kept talking, Harold came around.

**SUPERFLUOUS** adj. *extra, unnecessary; or, wasteful*

Harold said, "Okay, just a few questions. First, and this is major, not *superfluous*, what are we going to do for two days? That camp barely has electricity, you know!" True, and electricity isn't exactly a *superfluous* item.

**OBSOLETE** adj. *out of date, not in use; outmoded, passé*

I'd forgotten that the camp's equipment was *obsolete*. Of course, I'd been thinking about the lake and the dock and the canoes, things that would never be *obsolete* for me.

**DIFFIDENT** adj. *hesitant, lacking confidence; unassertive*

"Well," I began *diffidently*, a new idea taking hold, "let's rough it, then. No electricity, no boom boxes—not one modern thing. Total nostalgia," I continued happily, my *diffident* attitude vanishing. "That wouldn't be pedestrian!"

## MEMORY FIX

Of course you remember. Write the words you don't know with their definitions. Say them aloud and THINK.

## FIND THE ODDBALL

In each word group, cross out the oddball, the one unrelated word or phrase.

1. proficient with language   fluent   skillful   articulate

2. dangerous   explosive   changeable   volatile   unstable

3. charming   smooth   richly flowing   mellifluous

4. unconfident   diffident   unsure   wary   unaggressive

5. hard to manage   pedestrian   naughty   defiant   unruly

## MATCHING

In column B, find two synonyms or phrases that explain each word in column A. Write them on the lines provided.

|  | **A** | **B** |
|---|---|---|
| _____ | 1. recalcitrant | prudent |
| _____ |  | unnecessary |
| _____ | 2. circumspect | outmoded |
| _____ |  | unimaginative |
| _____ | 3. diffident | refractory |
| _____ |  | striking |
| _____ | 4. obsolete | totally accurate |
| _____ |  | hesitant |
| _____ | 5. rigorous | productive |
| _____ |  | fertile |
| _____ | 6. prolific | wasteful |
| _____ |  | passé |
| _____ | 7. pedestrian | watchful |
| _____ |  | demanding |
| _____ | 8. conspicuous | unassertive |
| _____ |  | unruly |
| _____ | 9. superfluous | very noticeable |
| _____ |  | ordinary |

## FILL IN THE BLANKS

Select the best word from this chapter's word list to complete the meaning and logic of each sentence. Change any word as needed for grammatical correctness.

1. Obviously puzzled as to my meaning, yet trying not to laugh, Jeff gave me a _____ glance and waited for my reply.

2. The pilot maintained he could fly anything, even the most _____ propeller plane in the hangar.

3. As a result of the massive data compiled during that study, their conclusions are virtually _____.

4. A brisk walk is one traditional way of starting the day in a _____ way.

5. For the person who's done something _____, there's an old saying: "Confession is good for the soul."

6. Valiant soldiers are decorated for _____ bravery.

7. A typical European, _____ in at least two or three languages, puts most Americans to shame.

8. _____ outdoor programs like Outward Bound have proved to be effective at building self-esteem.

9. Janie's is the sweetest voice on earth, the only _____ one in the midst of that cacophony of noise.

10. A moody, _____ person is apt to erupt like Pinatubo.

**Answers for this chapter begin on page 211.**

---

aloof • partisan • demeanor • altruism • austere •
provincial • authoritarian • nonchalant • brusque •
contrite • conciliatory • spurious

---

**ALOOF** adj. *reserved or cool in manner; uninvolved, remote*
Nearly 200 years ago, Coleridge wrote: "*Aloof* with hermit-eye I scan /
The present works of present man— / A wild and dreamlike trade of
blood and guile, / Too foolish for a tear, too wicked for a smile." Looks
as if it's always been tough to remain *aloof* from the evil that people
keep creating.

**PARTISAN** adj. *strongly in favor, biased, prejudiced* n. *follower
or member*
In a country tired of *partisan* politics, the American electorate hungers
for representatives who will put the good of the country, not their
political party, first. Many voters feel that pure *partisan* voting is blind
voting.

**DEMEANOR** n. *manner of handling yourself; mien,
comportment, bearing*
Queens are often described as having a stately *demeanor*, and busy
officials have a bustling *demeanor*. Our *demeanor* is our body language
and a major clue to character.

**ALTRUISM** n. *unselfish giving for the benefit of others* Society
has some full-time *altruists*, like teaching nuns and priests or Peace
Corps volunteers, and now and then the rest of us are motivated by
*altruism*. Major religions are based on the *altruistic* concept that those
who give will receive.

**AUSTERE** adj. *reserved, grave, somber in manner; self-denying,
abstemious; restrained* n. **austerity**
People who devote their lives to others aren't self-indulgent, so the
altruistic life is often quite *austere*. One example of holy *austerity* is that
of the contemplative monks who work and mediate in silence, talking
only rarely.

---

**FID = faith**

infidel—*a disbeliever in some specific sense*
    declared him an *infidel* and banned him from the church

perfidy—*faithlessness, disloyalty; betrayal, treachery*
    hated for his *perfidy*
    what *perfidious* behavior

Also: **confide, confidence, fidelity, diffident, diffidence, affidavit, confidant** *(intimate, trusted friend)*

---

**PROVINCIAL** adj. *referring to the provinces, or country; unsophisticated; or, parochial, narrow* n. **provincial**
Abraham Lincoln was once scorned as a *provincial* fellow by those who equated sophistication with intelligence. That same error was made by the city mouse who thought his country cousin was a *provincial*.

**AUTHORITARIAN** adj. *favoring subservience or allegiance to an authority rather than personal independence or freedom*
Author Edmund Wilson said, "Marx and Engels, coming out of *authoritarian* Germany, tended to imagine socialism in *authoritarian* terms." Independent Americans, of course, are never very comfortable with *authoritarian* governments.

**NONCHALANT** adj. *casual, carefree, cool, unconcerned*
*Nonchalant* at first, our family shrugged and said, "Oh, well, we can probably live with a few bats in the attic." But that *nonchalance* vanished when we began to smell something.

---

**ERR = to wander**

erratic—*on no set course, wandering, nomadic; devious*
    the *erratic* path of the butterfly
    at *erratic* intervals

aberration—*eccentricity; an oddity, not the norm*
    signs of an *aberrant* mind
    the *aberrations* of a recluse

Also: **error, erroneous, errant, arrant** *(extreme)*

---

**BRUSQUE** adj. *curt, abrupt, blunt (unpleasant in effect)*
When I said I needed to get rid of some bats in our attic, the clerk at the bat and bird shop snapped *brusquely*, "You should appreciate bats." Put off by her *brusque* manner, I said I was crazy about them, but not in my house.

**CONTRITE** adj. *sorrowful or repentant for some wrong* n. contrition
We're going to evict the bats from our house if we can, and we will not feel *contrite*. Well, maybe we'll suffer a few momentary pangs of *contrition*, but the bats can move to a nearby belfry.

**CONCILIATORY** adj. *reconciling, appeasing, pacifying (to improve relations)* v. conciliate
As a *conciliatory* gesture to the bats, I opened the louvers on the belfry of our church, advertising its desirability as a bat residence. I don't mind *conciliating* bats, who consume zillions of annoying bugs and mosquitoes.

**SPURIOUS** adj. *false, fake, though appearing legitimate; forged (as "a spurious passport")*
Opening the louvers to promote our church belfry as a home for the bats was not *spurious* advertising, because bats have always liked belfries. Generally speaking, though, the world of advertising generates a fair number of *spurious* claims.

## MEMORY FIX
Very near the end now. . . . Write down each word you don't know well; write definitions for each. Say them aloud.

## FILL IN THE BLANKS
From the new words in this chapter, select the one that best completes the meaning and logic of each phrase. Use the correct form of each word.

1. moved with the regal _____ of a Paris model

2. tossed his head _____ as if it didn't matter to him

3. ordered us to leave in a most _____ manner

4. Vidkun Quisling, a traitor whose _____ resulted in his surname becoming a word

5. following the wild, _____ path of the fleeing rabbit

6. apologizing for the omission with a sincere, _____ smile

7. illegal immigrants entering the United States with _____ documents

8. made timid by her _____, forbidding countenance

9. a generous person, known for a life of _____

10. eager to make up, extending his hand in a _____ gesture

## WHO SAID THAT?

From the list below, choose the most likely speaker to go with each remark.

| | | |
|---|---|---|
| an infidel | a partisan | the brusque type |
| the provincial | the authoritarian | an austere person |
| an altruist | a perfidious one | a nonchalant one |

1. I have no need of jewelry or stylish clothes or elegantly prepared foods. The simple life suits me. _____

2. We don't have to deal with that out here where there's a mile between neighbors, you see? _____

3. Briefly, that's it. Don't get it? Tough. _____

4. I am my brother's keeper. _____

5. They aren't like us—not at all, no sir. Why they should be so different from us is beyond me. _____

6. I'm not wearing that thing over my face and walking meekly behind him; you can just forget it! _____

7. Just do what I said and don't ask questions.

_____

8. I leaked that information, and I'd do it again.

_____

9. No sweat. Don't let it bother you. _____

## TRUE OR FALSE

Read each sentence to see how the new words in this chapter are being used. Then mark **T** (true) or **F** (false) beside each one.

1. To Americans, cannibalism is more than a mere *aberration*.

_____

2. For the sake of our teachers, we should turn in assignments on an *erratic* basis. _____

3. Neutral nations avoid entanglements, remaining *aloof*. _____

4. After bopping your brother on the head, you should assume a *contrite demeanor* and apologize. _____

5. The psychologist who masters a *brusque* approach will be the most successful. _____

6. One of the better *conciliatory* lines is, "We'll make sure that doesn't happen again." _____

7. To think that only private schools can offer a good education is a *provincial* outlook. _____

8. A *bipartisan* committee will probably write the Republican platform for the next election. _____

**Answers for this chapter begin on page 212.**

# ON THE DARK SIDE

---

**negligence • deleterious • depravity • crass • morose • caustic • guile • clandestine • cynical • furtive • apprehension • decadence**

---

**NEGLIGENCE** n. *lack of a sensible amount of care; neglect, carelessness* adj. **negligent**
Having bats in your house is not a sign of *negligence*, as bats can enter through the tiniest of openings. Learning that we hadn't been *negligent* homeowners helped us to feel somewhat better about the bats in our attic.

**DELETERIOUS** adj. *causing harm or injury, maybe in a very subtle way; maybe pernicious (deadly)*
We began to fret about the *deleterious* effects the bats might have on our house. One especially *deleterious* result of their invasion was the steady accumulation of bat guano.

**DEPRAVITY** n. *a state of corruption, perversion, or evil* adj. **depraved**
Grinning, Dad said, "I suggest we bag that stuff and sell it for fertilizer . . . if you don't think that's too *depraved*." Hearing our quite well-mannered father link himself to *depravity* made us hoot with laughter.

**CRASS** adj. *utterly lacking in taste or discrimination*
"I hate to sound *crass*," Mom interrupted, "but what do you think we could get for a bag of bat poo?" Coming from her, that was a *crass* remark, all right, but awfully funny.

**MOROSE** adj. *very gloomy or sullen in manner*
Amy stared *morosely* at the floor. Finally she said, "Look at me, troops. This is a depressed person wearing a *morose* face because we've got a real problem and you're all acting wacko!"

---

### BEL/BELL = war

**belligerent**—*combative, liking to start fights, bellicose*
 a *belligerent* attitude
 historically *belligerent* nations

**rebellious**—*resisting or opposing authority, refractory, recalcitrant*
 a *rebellious* attitude that always led to trouble

Also: **rebel, rebellion, antebellum** *(before the Civil War)* [And also **bell = beauty**—*belle, embellish*]

---

**CAUSTIC** adj. *biting, incisive, cutting, corrosive*
That was a pretty *caustic* approach for Amy, but her bedroom is right under the bats' roosting area. I guess I'd have a few *caustic* comments myself if my room were that close to the bat colony.

**GUILE** n. *trickery or deceit; deceptive cunning; duplicity*
Eventually, our family agreed that, although we liked bats and benefited from their insect-eating prowess, we would use every bit of *guile* we had to evict them. No strangers to cunning, bats are *guileful* creatures themselves at times.

**CLANDESTINE** adj. *secret, surreptitious*
Of course, I had already made a *clandestine* trip to our church belfry to open the louvres wider, hoping to lure the bats into the belfry. I'd been deliberately *clandestine* about my mission at church, because it sounded weird.

---

### VERS/VERT = to turn

**diverge**—*to alter a course; to go apart from one point; to differ in opinion; to deviate; to swerve*
 *diverging* rays of sunlight
 attitude *diverged* from the norm

**diverse**—*unlike, different*
 went their *diverse* ways
 several *diverse* opinions on that

Also: **revert, overt, covert, versatile, inadvertent, divert, diversion, perverse, controversy, extrovert, introvert**

---

**CYNICAL** adj. *distrustful of human nature; pessimistic, even misanthropic*
"I hate to be *cynical*," Dad said, "but how do you know that our bats will want to move to a belfry?" Of course I didn't know, and I was having deeply *cynical* thoughts myself about our ability to convince the bats to move out.

**FURTIVE** adj. *on the sly, in secret; surreptitious; stolen*
I zipped upstairs for a *furtive* peek at my old encyclopedia. Reading those basic bat facts again gave me an idea. There would be another *furtive* trip, I decided, this time to the bats' attic home, with an ultrasound device in hand.

**APPREHENSION** n. *a foreboding of something bad;·or, legal arrest*
Wishing I felt less *apprehension*, I prayed that the bats would move away from the electronic jamming of their radar. And what if they didn't? I waited *apprehensively* for the worst—Dad's call to an exterminator— but bats are smart, and ours soon moved next door to the belfry.

**DECADENCE** n. *decline and decay; deterioration*
We didn't have a totally *decadent* party after the bats left; I mean, we didn't really fall apart, but it was a loud, late party. Our neighbors made some not-too-subtle comments about how noisy it must have been in old, *decadent* Rome.

## MEMORY FIX
For the last time! Write down each word you don't know well along with a definition for each. Say them aloud.

## WORDS IN CONTEXT
Write the meanings of the words in italics on the lines provided.

1.  Arranging a *clandestine* meeting with the current love of your life is okay, but if you plan a *furtive* meeting, I'll be *apprehensive*, because *furtive* has more negative connotations.

    _____     _____

    _____     _____


2.  It's no surprise to learn that a *depraved* lifestyle has *deleterious* effects on health. _____     _____

3. History tells us that the *decadence* of Rome led to its decline.

   _____

4. Stung by several of his *caustic* remarks, I belatedly reminded myself that the fellow was a well-known *cynic*.

   _____    _____

5. Although Americans are obviously obsessed with money, it is considered by some to be a *crass* topic. _____

6. Is there such a thing as a purely *guileless* soul? _____

7. Mouth set in a *rebellious* pout, he remained silent.

   _____

8. After I accused him of gross *negligence*, he turned to me and sneered *morosely*, "So what?"

   _____    _____

## MATCHING SYNONYMS

Match the words in column A with their synonyms or definitions in column B.

|  | A | B |
|---|---|---|
| _____ | 1. clandestine | in poor taste |
| _____ | 2. diverge | foreboding |
| _____ | 3. caustic | deterioration |
| _____ | 4. diverse | pessimistic |
| _____ | 5. apprehension | deceit |
| _____ | 6. decadence | secret |
| _____ | 7. crass | biting, corrosive |
| _____ | 8. belligerent/ bellicose | to go apart |
| _____ | 9. guile | different |
| _____ | 10. cynical | spoiling for a fight |

## RHYME TIME

Add what is needed from this chapter's list of words to these varied bits of poetry, some wonderful, some corny.

1. The English teacher's face was long and _____.
   "Oh why," she cried, "are my writers verbose?"

2. "Macavity, Macavity, there's no one like Macavity,
   For he's a fiend in feline shape, a monster of

   _____."

   From *Old Possum's Book of Practical Cats,* T. S. Eliot

3. Cartoon cat Tom assumes a(n) _____ air,
   And we know he's tiptoeing toward Jerry's lair.

4. He said, "Let me at him," with a(n) _____ grin,
   Laced up his boxing gloves and waded in.

5. "Two roads _____ in a yellow wood," begins
   one of the most famous pieces of poetry ever written, by Robert
   Frost. Beginning at one place, the two roads followed a different
   path, and Frost "took the one less traveled by." Remember?

**Answers for this chapter begin on page 212.**

# LISTS 26–30 REVIEW

Yahoo, the last review! Read each group of words in lists 26 to 30 aloud and think of what each word means. Now you're ready for this final review.

## ANALOGIES

Circle the one word pair in each list below that expresses the same relationship as the pair in capital letters.

**1. DOCUMENT : SPURIOUS**
- (A) flight : erratic
- (B) nation : decadent
- (C) outline : diverse
- (D) passport : false
- (E) effort : futile

**2. RESOURCES : DEPLETE**
- (A) supplies : facilitate
- (B) health : enervate
- (C) strength : exhaust
- (D) force : coerce
- (E) energy : assail

**3. CARPING : ALIENATION**
- (A) apprehension : foreboding
- (B) perfidy : aberration
- (C) acrimony : conciliation
- (D) partisanship : rebellion
- (E) negligence : decadence

**4. MISANTHROPE : CYNICAL**
- (A) pedestrian : obsolete
- (B) stoic : impassive
- (C) altruist : unassailable
- (D) philanthropist : nonchalant
- (E) zany : depraved

**5. SUBTLE : COVERT**
- (A) flagrant : conspicuous
- (B) latent : innate
- (C) furtive : crass
- (D) reprehensible : bizarre
- (E) austere : provincial

**6. PARTISAN : ALOOF**
- (A) judge : perceptive
- (B) infidel : loyal
- (C) rebel : affluent
- (D) colonel : rigorous
- (E) buyer : urbane

# MATCHING ANTONYMS

Match the words in column A with their opposites in column B.

| | A | B |
|---|---|---|
| _____ | 1. reprehensible | deleterious |
| _____ | 2. urbane | belittle |
| _____ | 3. candid | learned, acquired |
| _____ | 4. bolster | docile |
| _____ | 5. salutary | vital |
| _____ | 6. recalcitrant | laudable |
| _____ | 7. innate | conciliatory |
| _____ | 8. austerity | self-absorption |
| _____ | 9. superfluous | coerce |
| _____ | 10. acrimonious | provincial |
| _____ | 11. cajole | guileful |
| _____ | 12. altruism | self-indulgence |

# MATCHING

Circle the two words or phrases that best explain the meaning of each numbered word in bold type.

1. **fluent**

   orally skilled   verbose   swiftly flowing   graceful   polite

2. **latent**

   delayed   recent   potential   dormant   lost

3. **diffident**

   unassertive   strange   unusual   hesitant   argumentative

4. **contrite**

   boring   banal   remorseful   repentant   angry

5. **crass**

   gross   mean-spirited   tasteless   thoughtless   grasping

6. **furtive**

    surreptitious  illegal  superstitious  clandestine  forbidden

7. **acute**

    perceptive  charming  geometric  pointed  painful

8. **infer**

    popular pine tree  conclude  resume  deduce  suppose

9. **prosaic**

    pedestrian  enervating  tiring  everyday  unpoetic

10. **authoritarian**

    democratic  autocratic  despotic  rigorous  demonic

## FILL IN THE BLANKS

From the list below, select the best word to complete each sentence. Alter the words as required for grammatical correctness.

| | | | | |
|---|---|---|---|---|
| erratic | static | facilitate | aberration | caustic |
| advocate | diverse | rigorous | circumspect | prolific |
| morose | denounce | futile | bellicose | |

1. Trained as a biochemist, Isaac Asimov was one of our century's most versatile, _____ authors, publishing over 300 books on _____ topics.

2. The dynamics of a changing community assure that almost nothing within it will remain _____ for long.

3. Can anything be done to _____ the use of high-speed rail in this country, or is that a _____ cause, doomed to fail?

4. "I'm afraid the old dog's _____ heartbeat is the norm for him now, not just a temporary _____," said the vet.

5. It's one thing to be _____, but Mother's Aunt Aggie is so unswervingly prudent that she never has any fun.

6. You can wipe that _____, down-in-the-mouth look off your face with some _____ exercise that enlivens mind and body.

7. Always quick to criticize, the media have enjoyed _____ the new administration with one _____ comment after another.

8. Some boys have such a _____ nature that counselors _____ sports like boxing to help them vent their aggression.

## TRUE OR FALSE

Read the sentences below to see if the words in the past five chapters are being used correctly. Then mark **T** (true) or **F** (false) beside each one.

1. Someone exhibiting a *nonchalant demeanor* in the presence of highly *volatile* substances manipulated by a *zany* fanatic can indeed be characterized as cool. _____

2. It helps if the instructions to your VCR are somewhat *opaque*. _____

3. *Proliferation* of nuclear weapons *exacerbates* an already *apprehensive* attitude on the part of many. _____

4. You can be *enervated* even by an *incipient* illness. _____

5. You're apt to give a *bizarre* outfit a *quizzical* look. _____

6. *Brusque* funeral home directors do a thriving business. _____

**Answers for this review lesson begin on page 213.**

## WHAT YOU ALREADY KNOW—A QUICK REVIEW

### Lesson A, Memory Check (p. 10)

Prefix A/AN; Meaning: *not, without*; Examples: atheist, anomaly, atypical

Prefix AB/ABS; Meaning: *from, away*; Examples: absent, abdicate, abstain

Prefix DIS/DI/DIFF; Meaning: *away, apart, negative*; Examples: disparate, dissuade, difference

Prefix ANTE/ANTI; Meaning: *before, previous*; Examples: anteroom, anticipate

Prefix BENE; Meaning: *good, well*; Examples: benefit, benevolent, beneficial

Prefix CIRCU; Meaning: *around*; Examples: circumference, circumvent, circuit

Prefix DI/DIA; Meaning: *across, apart, through*; Examples: diameter, dialogue, dilate

Prefix ANTI; Meaning: *against, opposing*; Examples: antisocial, antidote, antipathy

Prefix CO/COL/COM; Meaning: *with, together*; Examples: cooperate, concede, concur

### Lesson B, Memory Check 1 (p. 12)

1. outside 2. mixed, not all the same 3. *in*decent and *in*substantial 4. playing it for all you're worth, to the *max*imum 5. bad; *maleficent* literally means *make bad* 6. changes or alters

### Lesson B, Memory Check 2 (p. 14)

Prefix MICRO; Meaning: *small*; Examples: microbe, microphone, microcosm

Prefix PRE; Meaning: *before*; Examples: predict, prefix, preliminary

Prefix ORTH; Meaning: *straight, right*; Examples: orthopedic, orthodox

Prefix PER; Meaning: *through, throughout*, or *completely, wrongly*; Examples: permeate, permit

Prefix PERI; Meaning: *around, near*; Examples: periscope, perimeter, periphery

Prefix PRO; Meaning: *for, forward, before, forth, favoring*; Examples: promote, provision

Prefix POST; Meaning: *after, following*; Examples: postpone, postmortem, posterior

Prefix RE/RETRO; Meaning: *back, again*; Examples: recoil, retreat, retroactive

Prefix OMNI/PAN; Meaning: *all, entire*; Examples: omnipresent, pantheon, pandemic

### Lesson B, Memory Check 3 (p. 16)

1. *se*parated 2. afar 3.*sub*marine 4. Super, super, *sur*pass 5. *syn*chronizing, *together*

# LIST 1 (p. 17)

## Fill In the Blanks

1. acquiese 2. condone 3. effaced 4. chastise 5. concurred 6. laud 7. amass
8. augment 9. digress 10. cursory 11. digressive 12. coalesced 13. disperse
14. disperse 15. emitted

## Analogies

**1.** (C) chastise : misbehavior :: laud : success

Implied comparison. Behaviors linked to the verbs most commonly associated with them.

**2.** (E) footprints : efface :: record : obliterate

Implied comparison. Two human traces and ways in which they are commonly ''wiped out,'' completely eradicated.

**3.** (B) acquiese : yielding :: disperse : scattering

Inherent linkage. *Acquiesce* always implies giving way or yielding, just as *disperse* always refers to scattering in some sense.

**4.** (A) path : stray :: lecture : digress

Implied comparison. To leave a path is to *stray* off it, just as leaving the main point of a lecture is to *digress*. These words are linked by usage as well as by meaning.

**5.** (C) pardon : offense :: condone : error

Implied comparison. An *offense*, if excused, is said to be *pardoned*, whereas an *error*—less serious in nature—is said to be *condoned* if someone overlooks it or makes excuses.

## Matching

1. (B) assent, (D) yield 2. (A) utter, (B) voice 3. (B) chastise, (C) scold
4. (A) forerunner, (D) harbinger 5. (B) accumulate, (C) gather 6. (A) enlarge,
(B) add to 7. (B) strew around, (D) disseminate 8. (A) join, (C) come together
9. (B) wear away, (C) erase 10. (A) sketchy, (D) hasty

# LIST 2 (p. 23)

## True or False

1. F 2. T 3. F 4. F 5. T 6. F 7. T 8. F 9. T 10. T

## Matching

1. d 2. g 3. l 4. h 5. i 6. c 7. e 8. k 9. a 10. j 11. b 12. f

## Fill In the Blanks
1. banal and hackneyed (and maybe also trite and full of platitudes!) 2. concise, succinct, laconic, terse, and pithy 3. hyperbole 4. platitude, banality 5. equivocal

# LIST 3 (p. 28)
## Fill In the Blanks
1. insurgents 2. hypocritical 3. hedonistic 4. glutton 5. inexorable 6. charlatans (possibly hypocrites or sycophants) 7. skeptical 8. despot 9. heretic 10. zealot 11. miser 12. bigoted 13. sycophant 14. verify

## Rhyme Time
1. Gluttony (Yes, Orson Welles really said this.) 2. fanatic 3. oracle 4. skeptic 5. sycophant 6. hedonist 7. inexorable 8. aver

## Matching
1. (m) Scrooge, (c) hoarder 2. (d) nonbeliever, (p) one who differs 3. (f) tyrant, (h) autocrat 4. (i) fake, fraud; (g) impostor 5. (a) bias, (k) prejudice 6. (o) confirm, (b) corroborate 7. (l) fanatical, (n) overeager 8. (j) one in revolt, (e) rebel

# LIST 4 (p. 33)
## Fill In the Blanks
1. superficiality 2. listlessness 3. fervor 4. profusion 5. vulnerability 6. indulgence 7. unobtrusiveness 8. uniformity

## True or False
1. T  2. F  3. F  4. T  5. T  6. T  7. T  8. T  9. F  10. T

## Matching Antonyms
1. (a) irrelevant, (m) inappropriate 2. (d) restrained, (n) stingy 3. (e) inconsistent, (p) varied 4. (f) exhilarating, (k) restful 5. (g) thorough, (l) deeply serious 6. (b) weak, (q) ineffective 7. (j) critical, (o) unforgiving (maybe also n. stingy) 8. (h) bouncy, (s) enthusiastic 9. (i) gregarious, (r) friendly 10. (t) conspicuous, (c) aggressive

# LIST 5 (p. 38)
## Matching
1. (B) exceedingly particular, (C) meticulous 2. (C) disapprove of, (D) regret 3. (A) prideful, (D) overbearing 4. (A) stoop, (B) unbend 5. (B) scorn, (C) disdain 6. (C) belittle, (D) mock or jeer 7. (A) smug, (B) self-satisfied 8. (B) privilege, (D) right 9. (A) scoff at, (C) ridicule 10. (B) minimize, (C) decry

## Words in Context

1. openly and disdainfully proud 2. showy, self-important, pompous 3. disdainfully superior, scornful, proud 4. scorn, contempt 5. scorned, strongly disapproved of 6. scornful, disparaging, belittling, negatively critical 7. snootily and rather scornfully coming down to another's level (may be very subtle or quite open) 8. right, privilege 9. an ''Oh, don't mind me'' attitude that is modest and self-effacing, intended to put that person in the background 10. smugness, self-satisfaction

## Analogies

1. (D) Napoleon : arrogance :: Twain : satire

   Person linked to well-known skill or trait.

2. (B) remark : disparaging :: attitude : scoffing

   Implied comparison. A remark that puts another down is a *disparaging* remark, just as an attitude that puts another down is *scoffing*.

3. (D) pride : hauteur :: satisfaction : complacency

   Escalating degree. Extreme pride is *hauteur* just as the extreme of satisfaction is *complacency*.

4. (E) derision : ridicule :: scorn : contempt

   Analogy of definition or main characteristic. *Derision* always involves or means *ridicule*, just as *scorn* implies *contempt* (by definition).

# REVIEW, LISTS 1–5
## Find the Oddball

1. heretic 2. hauteur 3. insist 4. nasty 5. hyperbole 6. interesting 7. provoke 8. inevitable 9. hedonist 10. hackneyed

## True or False

1. T 2. F 3. F 4. F 5. F 6. F 7. T 8. T 9. T 10. F

## Find the Synonym

1. equivocal 2. to concur 3. banal 4. listless 5. to chastise 6. charlatan 7. to condone 8. precursor 9. inexorable 10. grueling 11. profuse 12. potent

## Who Said That?

1. orator 2. raconteur 3. glutton 4. recluse 5. skeptic 6. despot 7. insurgent 8. scoffer 9. heretic 10. equivocator 11. interrogator 12. deprecator

## Matching
1. to come together 2. to praise 3. superficial or hasty 4. pompous language
5. banality 6. to declare firmly 7. accidental 8. to ridicule 9. right or privilege
10. disdain, scorn 11. to increase 12. to scatter or fan out 13. to obliterate; wear
away 14. lenient 15. continuous

# LIST 6 (p. 48)

## Rhyme Time
1. raze 2. immutable 3. posit 4. meander 5. mutant
## Matching
1. (A) blemish, (C) spoil 2. (C) relieve, (D) alleviate 3. (B) efface, (C) wipe out 4.
(A) snub, (D) reject 5. (B) collect, (D) accumulate 6. (A) cloud over, (B) conceal
7. (C) study carefully, (D) examine 8. (B) wander, (C) ramble 9. (C) soothe, (D)
appease 10. (B) tear down, (D) demolish 11. (A) invalidate, (D) negate 12. (B)
mind or obey, (C) consider

## Substitution
1. heed 2. proponent 3. marred 4. obscured 5. mitigate 6. rebuffed 7. placate
8. perusing 9. nullify 10. garnered

# LIST 7 (p. 53)
## Fill In the Blanks
1. virtuosos or virtuosi 2. quandary 3. lucid 4. parsimonious 5. zenith 6. Torpor
7. nostalgia 8. volition 9. reticent 10. temerity

## Matching Antonyms
1. confidence 2. bombast 3. nadir 4. hyperactive 5. timidity 6. to obscure
7. order 8. beginner 9. descendant 10. generosity

## Find the Oddball
1. assortment 2. angle 3. niece 4. instinct 5. temperament 6. quest 7. betrayal
8. transparent 9. fear 10. quaintness

# LIST 8 (p. 58)
## Find the Synonym
1. formidable 2. profound 3. untenable 4. tenet 5. resilient 6. astute
7. meticulous 8. tenacious 9. alleviate

## True or False

1. F  2. T  3. F  4. T  5. T  6. F  7. T  8. T  9. T  10. F  11. F

## Analogies

1. (C) lawyer : astute :: pathologist : painstaking

   Person linked to most desirable trait.

2. (D) profound : thoughtful :: sagacious : bright

   Descending degree. *Profound* is very deeply thoughtful just as *sagacious* is exceedingly bright.

3. (D) Supreme Court : sagacity :: muscles : resilience

   Noun linked to most critical quality, one that is the defining factor.

4. (E) formidable : defense :: redoubtable : warrior

   Noun linked to logical adjective. The best kind of defense is *formidable*, just as the best warrior is *redoubtable*.

# LIST 9 (p. 63)

## Word Analysis

1. good or mellow, jangly or jarring noise 2. optimist, pessimist 3. stringent, lax 4. Objective, subjective 5. concrete, abstract 6. burgeon, atrophy 7. affluent, indigent 8. levity, gravity 9. consecrated, desecrates 10. irrefutable, refuted 11. irresolute, resolute

## Using the Words

1. atrophy, burgeon 2. irrefutable, refutable 3. objective, subjective 4. desecrate, consecrate 5. abstract, concrete 6. lax, stringent 7. cacophony, euphony 8. optimism, pessimism 9. gravity, levity 10. resolute, irresolute

# LIST 10 (p. 69)

## Fill In the Blanks

1. irascible 2. rancor (perhaps rue or malice) 3. premonition 4. surreptitiously 5. tawdry 6. sullen 7. writhing 8. malice (rancor) 9. taciturn 10. servile 11. malice 12. rue

## Matching

1. self-reproach, guilty unease 2. forewarning, foreboding 3. slander, defame 4. quietly resentful, lowering 5. bitterness, old enmity 6. cheap, gaudy 7. secretive, deceptive 8. laconic, silent 9. subservient, abject 10. testy, choleric

## Rhyme Time

1. writhe 2. rue 3. admonished 4. malice 5. mediocre 6. mediate

# REVIEW, LISTS 6–10
## Find the Synonym
1. obscure 2. mitigate 3. immutable 4. respite 5. parsimonious 6. lucid 7. astute
8. abstract 9. burgeon 10. resolute 11. sacrilege 12. taciturn

## Analogies

1. (D) symphony : violins :: religion : tenets

   Part of a whole. Violins are a significant part of any *symphony*, just as various *tenets* are part of any religion.

2. (B) energy : torpor :: government : anarchy

   Opposites. Also, think of this sentence: Lacking energy, you have *torpor*; lacking government, you have *anarchy*.

3. (B) sin : remorseful :: mistake : rueful

   Implied comparison. If you commit a sin you feel *remorseful*, just as making a mistake causes you to feel *rueful*.

4. (E) past : nostalgia :: future : optimism

   Implied comparison. We typically view the past with *nostalgia*, just as we view the future with *optimism*. (C) is a weak choice because not everyone views the present with pessimism.

5. (C) mediate : sage :: elucidate : teacher

   Specific person linked to one major function inherent in that position. A sage is well qualified to *mediate*, just as a teacher is well qualified to *elucidate*.

6. (C) battle : trepidation :: enemy : rancor

   Implied comparison. We typically view a battle with *trepidation* just as we view an enemy with *rancor*.

## Matching Antonyms
1. heir 2. indigent 3. levity 4. lax 5. rigidity 6. malicious 7. irritate 8. scan
9. ignore 10. temerity 11. silly 12. even-tempered

## Fill In the Blanks
1. garner 2. meticulous 3. reticent 4. rebuffed 5. razed, obliterating 6. volition
7. quandary 8. irrefutable 9. proponents 10. virtuosos 11. tenacious 12. zenith

# LIST 11 (p. 78)
## Substitution
1. rejuvenate 2. vacillating 3. implying 4. temper 5. acclaim 6. venerate or revere
7. scrutinized 8. disclaim 9. sanctions, sanction (v.) 10. waived

## Find the Oddball

1. sponge 2. twist 3. flinch 4. dankness 5. implied 6. deter 7. urge 8. discourage 9. relegate 10. reject

## True or False

1. F  2. T  3. T  4. T  5. T  6. F  7. F  8. T

# LIST 12 (p. 83)

## Fill In the Blanks

1. criteria 2. delineate 3. dearth, prodigious (or copious) 4. minced 5. magnanimously

## Matching

1. (B) briefness, (D) conciseness 2. (C) outline, (D) portray accurately 3. (B) immense, (C) enormous 4. (A) scarcity, (C) paucity 5. (A) fleeting, (B) transient 6. (C) scanty, (D) skimpy 7. (B) unnecessary, (D) superfluous 8. (A) generous in spirit, (D) big-hearted

## Words in Context

1. any standard used for making judgments 2. a person of rank, power, or influence 3. fading fast, like vapor 4. in great and plentiful supply 5. very, very tiny 6. talk indirectly or in any confusing way; mincing words with someone is failing to be direct 7. briefness, succinctness 8. big-hearted, forgiving 9. unnecessary, superfluous 10. enormous, huge, impressive

## Matching Antonyms

1. enduring, long-lived 2. scanty, minuscule, also meager 3. plentiful amount, copious 4. superabundance, plentiful amount 5. tiny, minuscule, also meager

# LIST 13 (p. 89)

## Matching

1. unwanted or unneeded 2. unavoidable 3. opportunistic 4. strenuous 5. insanely idealistic 6. of doubtful authorship 7. commonplace 8. abominable, appalling

## Fill In the Blanks

1. predilection 2. eclectic 3. prodigal 4. legitimate 5. legislate 6. negligible 7. ironic 8. aesthetic

## Analogies

1. (D) daydreaming : quixotic :: cleaning house : mundane

   Activity linked to most logical descriptive adjective.

2. (E) bad : heinous :: difficult : arduous

Escalating degree. Bad is much less awful than *heinous*, just as difficult is much less demanding than *arduous*.

3. (B) apocryphal : legend :: fictitious : fable

Logical literary description linked to literary genre. Both legends and fables are apt to be made up—fictitious.

## Find the Antonym

1. apocryphal 2. quixotic 3. avoidable 4. desired 5. significant 6. aversion 7. haphazard 8. noble 9. customary 10. mundane 11. parsimonious 12. impractical

# LIST 14 (p. 94)

## Substitution

1. rhetorical 2. garble 3. diatribe 4. satire 5. blasphemy 6. garrulous 7. jargon 8. indicted 9. tirade 10. slander

## True or False

1. T 2. F 3. F 4. T 5. T 6. F 7. T

## Matching

1. wordy, garrulous 2. defame, slander (or dishonor or malign) 3. fretful, petulant 4. corrosive, caustic 5. command, legal order 6. questioning, curious 7. defame, dishonor (or malign)

# LIST 15 (p. 99)

## Words In Context

1. *indifferent* = unconcerned, aloof, unattached, uninterested 2. *capitulate* = yield or give in to what another wants 3. *defer* = put off until another time 4. *innocuous* = harmless 5. *languor* = sluggishness, lethargy 6. *stagnant* = stale, unmoving, inactive 7. *deduced* = concluded or inferred through reasoned thought

## Matching

1. (A) vary up or down, (D) come and go 2. (B) suspicious, (C) of doubtful quality 3. (C) wishy-washiness, (D) indecision 4. (A) hesitant, (B) unsure 5. (B) languorous, (D) torpid 6. (C) indefinite, (D) uncertain 7. (A) avoid, (C) circumvent 8. (B) promoting, (D) assisting 9. (C) permeate, (D) diffuse throughout

## Find the Synonym

1. evade 2. defer 3. languor 4. innocuous 5. stagnant 6. indifferent 7. tentative 8. capitulate

# REVIEW, LISTS 11–15
## Analogies

1. (C) vacillate : ambivalence :: blaspheme : irreverence

   Implied comparison. To *vacillate* is to reveal *ambivalence*, just as to *blaspheme* shows *irreverence*.

2. (D) ephemeral : duration :: meager : amount

   Words of measurement in implied comparison. Something that is only *ephemeral* in duration won't last long, just as something *meager* in amount won't last very long either.

3. (B) satire : irony :: tirade : criticism

   Part of a whole or related by definition, maybe even implied comparison! Think of this sentence: *Irony* is basic to *satire*, just as *criticism* is the basis of a *tirade*.

4. (E) reputation : slander :: communication : garble

   Implied comparison. To *slander* a reputation ruins it, just as to *garble* a bit of communication ruins it.

5. (B) spirit : magnanimous :: effort : prodigious

   Relationship of size. A big spirit is a *magnanimous* one, just as a big effort is a *prodigious* one.

## Matching

1. (B) give way to 2. (A) hint 3. (C) foil 4. (D) sharpen 5. (A) natural preference 6. (B) demanding 7. (B) fictitious 8. (D) languor 9. (C) beyond question 10. (A) superfluous

## Find the Oddball

1. announce 2. adjudicate 3. admonish 4. speech 5. jargon 6. dirty 7. menial 8. vapor 9. unreal 10. goal-oriented 11. supply 12. adorable

## Fill In the Blanks

1. waive 2. tentative 3. conducive 4. copious, prodigious 5. prodigal 6. eclectic 7. aesthetic 8. fluctuated, negligible 9. pervasive, deduced 10. vitriolic, vilified 11. diatribe, capitulated, innocuous 12. saturated, clamoring

# LIST 16 (p. 108)

## Fill In the Blanks

1. enjoins 2. undermined 3. extorting 4. solicitous 5. emanates 6. rescinded 7. extricate 8. emulate 9. expedite 10. subjugating 11. relegate 12. enhances

## Rhyme Time

1. repudiate 2. hamper, relegated 3. rescind, enhance 4. squander 5. extort

## Matching

1. facilitate 2. squander 3. ask for 4. hamper 5. weaken gradually 6. seep out 7. forbid 8. try to equal 9. tortuous 10. repeal

# LIST 17 (p. 113)

## True or False

1. F   2. T   3. T   4. F   5. T   6. F   7. F   8. T   9. T   10. T

## Find the Oddball

1. price 2. honor 3. urgency 4. symbiosis 5. master 6. hackneyed 7. aloof

## Matching

1. sloth, idleness 2. mercy, lenience 3. a cleansing, a purging 4. wrong assumption, error 5. obstacle, impediment 6. paradox, irregularity 7. neophyte, novice 8. convivial, sociable 9. original, new 10. outstandingly bad, flagrant

# LIST 18 (p. 118)

## Find the Synonyms

1. frivolity 2. amiable 3. jocular (effervescent is okay) 4. dispassionate 5. apathetic 6. effervescent 7. serene 8. benign 9. amity 10. jocular

## Fill In the Blanks

1. benign or serene 2. extolled 3. placid 4. effervescence 5. ameliorate 6. frivolous 7. Blithe 8. assuage 9. elation 10. blithe, amiable, or maybe jocular; appease

## Find the Antonyms

1. downcast 2. effervescent 3. irritate 4. dispassionate 5. censure 6. frivolous 7. overwrought

# LIST 19 (p. 123)

## Words in Context

1. *unsavory* = unappetizing, unappealing, disgusting 2. *inflated* = puffed up, enlarged 3. *impotent* = powerless, ineffective 4. *partial* = biased, strongly disposed toward 5. *intangible* = not concrete, impalpable yet real 6. *auspicious* = favorable, boding well, propitious 7. *indiscriminate* = randomly, without

discrimination 8. *dissent* = disagreement 9. *autocrat* = despot, tyrant, dictator 10. *aristocracy* = ruling class; qualified ones

## True or False

1. F  2. T  3. F  4. F (maybe T!)  5. T  6. T (You can guess this one even if you don't know for sure.)  7. T  8. F  9. T  10. T

## LIST 20 (p. 128)
### Substitution

1. didactic 2. gullible 3. incorrigible 4. inane, wanton 5. tedious 6. docile, pompous 7. officious 8. petty 9. dogmatic 10. insipid

### Matching

1. inconstant, changeable 2. naive, ingenuous 3. dull, flavorless 4. pedantic, preachy 5. delinquent, recalcitrant 6. witless, insipid 7. unchecked, inhumane 8. established, traditional 9. compliant, tractable 10. interfering, impertinent

### Find the Oddball

1. ugly 2. unsavory 3. biased 4. theoretical 5. moderate 6. fickle

# REVIEW LISTS 16–20
# ANALOGIES

1. (D) reasoning : fallacious :: judgment : biased

    Implied comparison. The worst kind of reasoning would be *fallacious*, just as the worst kind of judgment would be *biased*.

2. (C) infamy : censure :: virtue : extol

    Cause and effect. Historically, we *censure* infamy, just as we *extol* virtue.

3. (E) pleasant : jocular :: contented : blithe

    Ascending degree.

4. (E) demagogue : sincerity :: neophyte : experience

    Person and missing trait. A *demagogue* usually lacks sincerity, just as a *neophyte* lacks experience.

5. (B) effervescent : elation :: deflated : repudiation

    Cause and effect. The result of elation is an *effervescent* feeling, just as the result of repudiation is a *deflated* feeling.

6. (E) confidence : undermine :: embankment : erode

    Implied comparison. Confidence can be *undermined* in the same way that an embankment is *eroded*. (Very similar processes although one is concrete, the other abstract.)

## Matching Antonyms

1. concrete 2. humble 3. carefully controlled 4. hinder 5. aggravate 6. ominous, foreboding 7. agreement 8. engrossing, absorbing 9. ineffective 10. disgrace 11. similarity 12. implicate

## Find Those Synonyms

1. hinder, impede 2. repeal, call back 3. enjoin, command 4. tortuous, crooked 5. novice, beginner 6. gregarious, amicable 7. vacillating, inconstant 8. assuage, conciliate 9. unfeeling, apathetic 10. insipid, empty

## Good Words Get Around

1. undermining 2. impartial 3. squander 4. alleviates 5. placid 6. frivolous 7. dogmatic 8. petty

# LIST 21 (p. 137)
## Fill In the Blanks

1. credulous 2. scrupulous 3. Steadfast 4. thrifty, prudence 5. pragmatist 6. exemplary 7. frugality, diligence, prudence, discretion, and thrift, plus probably pragmatism and steadfastness, too—eight virtues in all! 8. parochial (narrow) 9. solemnity, solemn 10. credibility, generic

## Add the Synonyms

1. frugal, sparing, provident 2. prudent, also modest 3. parochial 4. exemplary 5. scrupulous 6. steadfast, faithful 7. congenial, with kindred tastes

## True or False

1. T  2. F  3. T  4. F (probably)  5. F  6. F  7. T  8. T

# LIST 22 (p. 142)
## Substitution

1. intercede 2. oblivious 3. cryptic or enigmatic 4. hypothetical 5. chimerical 6. esoteric 7. karma 8. elusive 9. eccentric, precedent 10. chronic, utopia

## True or False

1. T  2. T  3. F  4. F  5. F  6. F  7. T

## Matching

1. without example, novel 2. perceptive, a seer 3. aberrational, odd 4. undecipherable, enigmatic 5. "out to lunch," clueless 6. intervene, mediate 7. repetitive, long-lasting 8. secondhand, substitutionary 9. ideal, perfect 10. fanciful, imaginary

# LIST 23 (p. 147)
## Fill-In Chart
1. *vindictive*; dic/dict = say; revengeful, *spiteful* 2. turbulent; turb = agitate; *seething, agitated* 3. *homogeneous*; hom = same, gen = kind; same or alike throughout 4. *animosity*; anim = spirit, soul; enmity, *hatred* 5. *haphazard*; hap = luck, chance; *unplanned, random* 6. *equanimity*; equ = equal, same; anim = spirit, soul; *evenness of disposition, balance* 7. virulent; virus = poison; *noted for fast, powerful, and often fatal progress (virulent disease)* 8. convivial; con = with; viv = life; *party-loving, lively* 9. *ubiquitous*; ubique = everywhere; *omnipresent* 10. precocious; pre = before; coquere = cooked; *mentally ahead of schedule, prematurely bright*

## Rhyme Time
1. voluminous 2. voracious, whimsical 3. ubiquitous, "viable" 4. unimpeachable 5. incongruous

## Word Analysis
1. precocious 2. incongruous 3. turbulent 4. voracious 5. whimsical 6. vindictive

# LIST 24 (p. 152)
## Fill In the Blanks
1. extenuating 2. iconoclast 3. unethical 4. kindle 5. elaboration 6. tacit 7. insidious 8. tenuous 9. unscathed 10. propensity

## Matching Antonyms
1. honorable 2. peripheral 3. kindle 4. elaborate 5. discord 6. deter 7. spoken 8. precipitate 9. careless 10. traditionalist

## Matching
1. caustic, highly critical 2. tendency, inclination 3. around the edge, auxiliary 4. lack of harmony, strife 5. barely perceptible, flimsy 6. discourage, inhibit 7. dangerously alluring, subtle 8. model, admired example 9. impetuous, headlong 10. persistent, most attentive

# LIST 25 (p. 157)
## Substitution
1. arbitrary 2. desultory 3. detrimental 4. flagrant 5. resigned 6. sporadic 7. capricious 8. blatant 9. inherently 10. incisive

## True or False
1. F  2. F  3. F  4. T  5. F  6. F

## Matching

1. logical, lucid 2. succinct, brief 3. roundabout, crafty 4. agreeable, well-suited
5. liable, receptive to 6. irrelevant, nonessential 7. inborn, natural 8. "loud,"
glaring 9. irregular, inconstant 10. despotic, impulsive

# REVIEW, LISTS 21–25
## Analogies

1. (D) time : anachronistic :: setting : incongruous

   Implied comparison. Something out of place in time is *anachronistic*, just
   as something out of place in a particular setting appears *incongruous*: it
   "doesn't fit."

2. (B) prophet : clairvoyant :: paradigm : exemplary

   Person related to most logical trait. A prophet should be *clairvoyant*, just
   as a *paradigm* should be elemplary.

3. (D) apparent : flagrant :: careful : assiduous

   Ascending degree. *Flagrant* is the extreme of apparent, just as *assiduous*
   is the extreme of careful.

4. (E) water : turbulent :: thought : incoherent

   Implied comparison. Churning water is *turbulent*, just as churning
   thought is *incoherent*.

5. (B) appetite : voracious :: apparel : voluminous

   Comparison of size. A big, impressive appetite is often termed *voracious*,
   just as noticeable clothing that billows about like sails on a ship is termed
   *voluminous*.

6. (A) extraneous : detail :: peripheral : issue

   Comparison of location or function. An unnecessary detail is *extraneous*,
   just as an unnecessary issue is *peripheral*.

## Find the Oddball

1. brilliant (others related by the root *gen*) 2. prophecy 3. pragmatic 4. running
5. hideous 6. fragile 7. elucidate 8. alternate 9. erroneous 10. indigent
11. inspired 12. reclusive

## Who Said That?

1. pious one 2. iconoclast 3. clairvoyant 4. eccentric 5. arbitrary one
6. pragmatist 7. credulous one 8. vindictive one 9. convivial soul

## Find the Synonyms
1. congenial, compatible 2. capricious, whimsical 3. desultory, haphazard 4. cryptic, enigmatic 5. frugal, thrifty 6. parochial, narrow 7. flimsy, tenuous 8. tacit, unspoken 9. propensity, tendency 10. chimerical, fanciful

## The Root of It All
1. ad*h*esive 2. *gen*ius 3. in*gen*uous 4. *gene* 5. en*gen*der 6. *gen*eric 7. disin*gen*uous 8. *cred*ible 9. inter*ced*e 10. *chron*ic 11. *anim*osity 12. equ*anim*ity 13. in*sid*ious 14. ex*ten*uating 15. in*cis*ors

# LIST 26 (p. 166)
## Fill In the Blanks
1. enervating, exhaust 2. belittle 3. carping 4. bolster 5. infer 6. perceptive 7. depleting (maybe exhausting) 8. incipient 9. facilitate 10. coercion, cajoled

## Antonyms
1. undermine 2. replenish 3. extol (also, acclaim) 4. terminal, final 5. hamper, hinder 6. dull, obtuse 7. energize 8. contain 9. acclaim (extol is okay)

## Switcheroo
1. estrangement 2. sponsorship, support 3. exhaustion 4. keenness 5. supporter 6. (rapid) multiplication 7. conclusion, deduction 8. negative criticism 9. wheedling, begging 10. force

# LIST 27 (p. 171)

## True or False
1. F  2. F  3. T  4. T  5. T  6. T  7. T  8. F  9. T  10. T

## Find the Synonyms
1. fantastic, shocking 2. unimaginative, ordinary 3. ludicrous, absurd 4. unchanging, stationary 5. sophisticated, suave 6. obtuse, dull-witted 7. very clever, insidious 8. dormant, potential 9. inborn, inherent 10. frank, guileless

## Substitution
1. prosaic, bizarre 2. urbane, opaque 3. candid, stoic, acrimonious 4. static (slang usage) 5. zany, futile

# LIST 28 (p. 177)

## Find the Oddball
1. skillful 2. dangerous 3. charming 4. wary 5. pedestrian

## Matching
1. refractory, unruly 2. prudent, watchful 3. unassertive, hestitant 4. outmoded, passé 5. totally accurate, demanding 6. productive, fertile 7. unimaginative, ordinary 8. very noticeable, striking 9. unnecessary, wasteful

## Fill In the Blanks
1. quizzical 2. obsolete 3. unassailable 4. salutary 5. reprehensible 6. conspicuous (a literal term, from actual citations) 7. fluent 8. Rigorous 9. mellifluous 10. volatile

# LIST 29 (P. 182)
## Fill In the Blanks
1. demeanor 2. nonchalantly 3. authoritarian 4. perfidy 5. erratic 6. contrite 7. spurious 8. austere 9. altruism 10. conciliatory

## Who Said That?
1. an austere person 2. the provincial 3. the brusque type 4. an altruist 5. a partisan 6. an infidel 7. the authoritarian 8. a perfidious one 9. a nonchalant one

## True or False
1. T   2. F   3. T   4. T   5. F   6. T   7. T   8. F

# LIST 30 (p. 187)
## Words in Context
1. *clandestine* = secret, surreptitious; *furtive* = on the sly, secret; *apprehensive* = worried, fearful of something bad 2. *depraved* = morally corrupt; *deleterious* = injurious, harmful 3. *decadence* = decay of moral standards and ethical conduct 4. *caustic* = biting, cutting, corrosive; *cynic* = person who distrusts human nature and views people pessimistically 5. *crass* = lacking good taste, crude, vulgar 6. *guileless* = lacking guile or trickery, ingenuous, open 7. *rebellious* = stubbornly resistant to authority 8. *negligence* = lack of care and attention, neglect; *morosely* = sullenly, gloomily

## Matching Synonyms
1. secret 2. to go apart 3. biting, corrosive 4. different 5. foreboding 6. deterioration 7. in poor taste 8. spoiling for a fight 9. deceit 10. pessimistic

## Rhyme Time
1. morose 2. depravity 3. furtive 4. bellicose (maybe belligerent, but it has too many syllables) 5. diverged

# REVIEW, LISTS 26–30
## Analogies

1. (D) document : spurious :: passport : false

   Implied comparison. A fake document is often termed *spurious*, just as a fake passport is usually termed *false*.

2. (C) resources : deplete :: strength : exhaust

   Implied comparison. To use up nearly all of your resources is to *deplete* them (common usage), just as using up nearly all of your strength is to *exhaust* it.

3. (E) carping : alienation :: negligence : decadence

   Cause and effect. *Carping* (repeated crisicism) often leads to alienation, just as negligence may lead to *decadence* (deterioration and decay).

4. (B) misanthrope : cynical :: stoic : impassive

   Person and most logical trait.

5. (A) subtle : covert :: flagrant : conspicuous

   Synonymous or by-definition relationship. Something *subtle* is by its nature a covert thing, just as something *flagrant* is bound to be conspicuous.

6. (B) partisan : aloof :: infidel : loyal

   Person and least likely trait/missing trait. A *partisan* will never remain aloof, just as an *infidel* will not remain loyal (to whatever group he once belonged to).

## Matching Antonyms

1. laudable 2. provincial 3. guileful 4. belittle 5. deleterious 6. docile 7. learned, acquired 8. self-indulgence 9. vital 10. conciliatory 11. coerce 12. self-absorption

## Matching

1. orally skilled, graceful 2. potential, dormant 3. unassertive, hesitant 4. remorseful, repentant 5. gross, tasteless 6. surreptitious, clandestine 7. perceptive, pointed 8. conclude, deduce 9. pedestrian, everyday 10.autocratic, despotic

## Fill In the Blanks

1. prolific, diverse 2. static 3. facilitate, futile 4. erratic, aberration 5. circumspect 6. morose, rigorous 7. denouncing, caustic 8. bellicose, advocate

## True or False

1. T 2. F 3. T 4. T 5. T 6. F

# INDEX OF WORDS AND ROOTS

The words and roots taught in this book are presented here in alphabetical order for ease of reference. Following each word is the number of the list, or chapter, in which it appears. Roots are in bold type.

aberration—29
abstract—9
acclaim—11
acquiesce—1
**ac/acr**—27
acrimonious—27
acute—27
admonish—10
advocate—26
aesthetic—13
affluent—9
**agr**—A Quick Review
alienate—26
alleviate—8
aloof—29
altruism-29
**am**—18
amass—1
ambiguous—15
ambivalence—15
ameliorate—18
amiable—18
amity—18
anachronism—22
anarchy—7
**anima**—23
animosity—23
anomaly—17
**anthrop**—27
antithesis—17
apathy—18
apocryphal—13
appease—18
apprehension—30
**aqua**—A Quick Review

arbitrary—25
**arch**—7
arduous—13
aristocracy—19
arrogant—5
articulate—2
assiduous—24
assuage—18
astute—8
atrophy—9
**aud/audit**—A Quick Review
augment—1
auspicious—19
austere—29
authoritarian—29
**auto**—A Quick Review
autocrat—19
aver—3

banal—2
belittle—26
**bel/bell** (war)—30
**bell** (beauty)—30
bellicose—30
belligerent—30
**bene**—8
benevolent—8
benign—18
biased—19
bigot—3
**bio**—A Quick Review
bizarre—27
blasphemy—14
blatant—25

blithe—18
bolster—26
bombast—2
brevity—12
brusque—29
burgeon—9

cacophony—9
cajole—26
candid—27
**cap/cip/cept**—26
capitulate—15
capricious—25
carp—26
catharsis—17
caustic—30
**ced/cess/cede**—22
censure—17
charlatan—3
chastise—1
chimera—22
**chron**—A Quick Review
chronic—22
**cid/cis**—25
circumspect—28
**civ**—A Quick Review
clairvoyant—22
**clam/claim**—11
clamor—11
clandestine—30
**claus/clud/clus**—4
clemency—17
coalesce—1
coerce—26

**cogn/cogni**—A Quick Review
coherent—25
compatible—25
complacent—5
conciliatory—29
concise—25
concrete—9
concur—1
condescend—5
condone—1
conducive—15
congenial—21
consecrate—9
consent—9
conspicuous—28
contempt—5
contrite—29
convivial—23
copious—12
**crac/crat**—19
crass—30
**cred**—21
credible—21
credulous—21
criterion—12
cryptic—22
**cur/curr/cours**—1
cursory—1
**cycl**—A Quick Review
cynical—30

dearth—12
decadence—30
deduce—15
defer—15
deflate—19
deleterious—30
delineate—12
**dem**—19
demagogue—19
demeanor—29
denounce—26
deplete—26
depravity—30

deprecate—5
deride—5
derogatory—5
desecrate—9
despot—3
desultory—25
deter—24
detrimental—25
devious—25
diatribe—14
**dic/dict**—14
didactic—20
diffident—28
digress—1
diligent—21
discerning—8
disclaim—11
discord—24
discreet—21
discriminate—19
disdain—5
disparage—5
disparity—17
dispassionate—18
disperse—1
disseminate—1
dissent—19
diverge—30
diverse—30
**doc/dact**—20
docile—20
**dog/dox**—20
dogmatic—20
dubious—15
**duc/duct**—15

eccentric—22
eclectic—13
edict—14
efface—1
effervescent—18
**ego**—A Quick Review
egregious—17
elaborate—24
elation—18

eloquent—2
elucidate—7
elusive—22
emanate—16
emit—1
emulate—16
enervate—26
engender—21
enhance—16
enigma—22
enjoin—16
ephemeral—12
equanimity—23
equivocal—2
**err**—29
erratic—29
esoteric—22
esteem—17
euphemism—2
euphony—9
evade—15
evanescent—12
exacerbate—27
exemplary—21
exhaust—26
expedient—13
expedite—16
explicit—11
extenuating—24
extol—18
extort—16
extraneous—25
extricate—16

facilitate—26
**fall/fals**—A Quick Review
fallacy—17
famous—19
fastidious—5
fervent—4
fickle—20
**fid**—29
flagrant—25
fledgling—17

**flu/flux/fluct**—28
fluctuate—15
fluent—28
formidable—8
fortuitous—4
frivolous—18
frugal—21
furtive—30
futile—27

garble—14
garner—6
garrulous—14
**ge/geo**—A Quick
    Review
**gen**—21
generic—21
germane—4
glutton—3
**gno**—A Quick Review
**graph/gram**—A Quick
    Review
gratuitous—13
gravity—9
**greg**—17
gregarious—17
grueling—4
guile—30
gullible—20

hackneyed—2
hamper—16
**hap**—23
haphazard—23
haughty—5
hedonist—3
heed—6
heinous—13
**her/hes**—25
heretic—3
hierarchy—7
hindrance—17
homogeneous—23
**hydr**—A Quick Review
hyperbole—2

hypocrite—3
hypothetical—22

iconoclast—24
impartial—19
imply—11
immutable—6
impassive—18
impotent—19
inane—20
inauspicious—19
incessant—4
incipient—26
incisive—25
incongruous—23
incorrigible—20
indefatigable—8
indict—14
indifferent—15
indigent—9
indiscriminate—19
indoctrinate—20
indolence—17
indulgent—4
inevitable—13
inexorable—3
infamous—19
infer—26
infidel—29
inflate—19
inherent—25
innate—27
innocuous—15
innovate—17
inquisitive—14
insidious—24
insipid—20
insurgent—3
intangible—19
intercede—22
irascible—10
irony—13
irrefutable—9
irresolute—9

jargon—14
jeopardy—17
jocular—18
judicious—8
**jug/junct/join**—16

karma—22
kindle—24

laconic—2
lampoon—2
languor—15
latent—27
laud—1
lax—9
**leg** (law)—13
**leg/lect/lig**—13
legacy—13
legitimate—13
lethargy—15
**lev**—8
leverage—8
levity—9
listless—4
**loc/loqu/log/ology**—2
loquacious—2
**lu/luc**—7
lucid—7

**magn**—12
magnanimous—12
magnate—12
**mal**—A Quick Review
malice—10
malign—10
mar (verb)—6
**mar** (sea)—A Quick
    Review
**mater**—A Quick
    Review
meager—12
meander—6
**medi**—10
mediate—10
mediocre—10